Spelman College
Atlanta, Georgia

Written by T. Murray

Layout and edits by Matt Hamman

Final Edits by Kelly Carey

Additional contributions by Omid Gohari, Joey Rahimi, and Luke Skurman

ISBN # 1-4274-0263-9
© Copyright 2006 College Prowler
All Rights Reserved
Printed in the U.S.A.
www.collegeprowler.com

Special Thanks To: Babs Carryer, Andy Hannah, LaunchCyte, Tim O'Brien, Bob Sehlinger, Thomas Emerson, Dave Lehman, Daniel Fayock, Chris Babyak, The Donald H. Jones Center for Entrepreneurship, Terry Slease, Jerry McGinnis, Bill Ecenberger, Idie McGinty, Kyle Russell, Jacque Zaremba, Larry Winderbaum, Roland Allen, Jon Reider, Team Evankovich, Lauren Varacalli, Abu Noaman, Mark Exler, Daniel Steinmeyer, Jared Cohon, Gabriela Oates, David Koegler, Ditto Documents Services, Meryl Sustarsic, Jaime Myers, Adam Burns, Carrie Petersen, Jon Skindzier, Alyson Pope, Jesse Rapsack, Heather Estes, Christina Koshzow, Chris Mason, and Glen Meakem.

Bounce-Back Team: Bianca Cooper, Latoya Pratt, and Sara Redd.

College Prowler®
5001 Baum Blvd.
Suite 750
Pittsburgh, PA 15213

Phone: 1-800-290-2682
Fax: 1-800-772-4972
E-Mail: info@collegeprowler.com
Web Site: www.collegeprowler.com

College Prowler® is not sponsored by, affiliated with, or approved by Spelman College in any way.

College Prowler® strives faithfully to record its sources. As the reader understands, opinions, impressions, and experiences are necessarily personal and unique. Accordingly, there are, and can be, no guarantees of future satisfaction extended to the reader.

© Copyright 2006 College Prowler. All rights reserved. No part of this work may be reproduced or transmitted in any form or by any means, including but not limited to, photocopy, recording, or any information storage and retrieval systems, without the express written permission of College Prowler®.

Welcome to College Prowler®

During the writing of College Prowler's guidebooks, we felt it was critical that our content was unbiased and unaffiliated with any college or university. We think it's important that our readers get honest information and a realistic impression of the student opinions on any campus—that's why if any aspect of a particular school is terrible, we (unlike a campus brochure) intend to publish it. While we do keep an eye out for the occasional extremist—the cheerleader or the cynic—we take pride in letting the students tell it like it is. We strive to create a book that's as representative as possible of each particular campus. Our books cover both the good and the bad, and whether the survey responses point to recurring trends or a variation in opinion, these sentiments are directly and proportionally expressed through our guides.

College Prowler guidebooks are in the hands of students throughout the entire process of their creation. Because you can't make student-written guides without the students, we have students at each campus who help write, randomly survey their peers, edit, layout, and perform accuracy checks on every book that we publish. From the very beginning, student writers gather the most up-to-date stats, facts, and inside information on their colleges. They fill each section with student quotes and summarize the findings in editorial reviews. In addition, each school receives a collection of letter grades (A through F) that reflect student opinion and help to represent contentment, prominence, or satisfaction for each of our 20 specific categories. Just as in grade school, the higher the mark the more content, more prominent, or more satisfied the students are with the particular category.

Once a book is written, additional students serve as editors and check for accuracy even more extensively. Our bounce-back team—a group of randomly selected students who have no involvement with the project—are asked to read over the material in order to help ensure that the book accurately expresses every aspect of the University and its students. This same process is applied to the 200-plus schools College Prowler currently covers. Each book is the result of endless student contributions, hundreds of pages of research and writing, and countless hours of hard work. All of this has led to the creation of a student information network that stretches across the nation to every school that we cover. It's no easy accomplishment, but it's the reason that our guides are such a great resource.

When reading our books and looking at our grades, keep in mind that every college is different and that the students who make up each school are not uniform—as a result, it is important to assess schools on a case-by-case basis. Because it's impossible to summarize an entire school with a single number or description, each book provides a dialogue, not a decision, that's made up of 20 different topics and hundreds of student quotes. In the end, we hope that this guide will serve as a valuable tool in your college selection process. Enjoy!

The College Prowler Team

SPELMAN COLLEGE
Table of Contents

By the Numbers............................ **1**	Drug Scene................................ **99**
Academics **4**	Campus Strictness **104**
Local Atmosphere **11**	Parking....................................... **108**
Safety & Security **17**	Transportation **114**
Computers.................................. **23**	Weather..................................... **120**
Facilities...................................... **28**	Report Card Summary **124**
Campus Dining.......................... **33**	Overall Experience **125**
Off-Campus Dining **39**	The Inside Scoop..................... **129**
Campus Housing **49**	Finding a Job or Internship **134**
Off-Campus Housing................ **58**	Alumnae **136**
Diversity...................................... **63**	Student Organizations............ **139**
Guys & Girls............................... **69**	The Best & Worst.................... **143**
Athletics...................................... **76**	Visiting....................................... **145**
Nightlife...................................... **82**	Words to Know........................ **149**
Greek Life **94**	

Introduction from the Author

To this day, I still feel warmth in my heart whenever I set foot on Spelman's campus. My college experience went beyond academic education by teaching me about life as an African American woman. Spelman has a reputation for educating the best and the brightest women from all over the country. When it was time for me to decide on a college, I had the good fortune of having an older sister who had attended the institution. As a 12-year-old, the concept of college was far from my mind. Four years later, as I listened to her stories, met her college friends, and visited the campus, I could see why she had chosen Spelman.

Spelman is an all-female institution and considered a Historically Black College/University (HBCU). HBCUs have a rich history, as many years ago they were among some of the only institutions where African Americans could enroll. As a place of higher learning, Spelman initially carved out its niche as a liberal arts institution, but it has grown to have a strong reputation in the sciences as well, and it even partners with other schools to give students the opportunity to seek engineering degrees. Academics are very important at Spelman, and the coursework is challenging. The school isn't concerned with pumping out thousands of degree-toting women each year so much as with the quality of the education students receive. At Spelman, you are part of a family, and the admissions process is selective in order to keep class sizes small. Don't look to Spelman as a school where you will learn and leave. Spelman provides every student with an experience as they journey to womanhood. There are traditions in which all students participate, and everything that takes place from the classroom to the student center is steeped in sisterhood. Spelman's goal is to educate and expand the minds of young women to see the world through their own eyes and the eyes of the women around them. They reach that goal your very first year.

Most high school students do not have the benefit of having an older sibling to be the guinea pig at the college they are thinking about attending. What they do have are books that spout out statistics and only give a glimpse at what the school looks like on paper and not the "personality" of the institution. On the following pages, you will be privy to a look at what it is really like to be a Spelman student, as told by those who are living the experience right now, as well as some who have graduated recently. Taking all of their experiences into account and the other information in this book will hopefully help you to make a more informed decision about whether or not Spelman is right for you.

T. Murray, Author
Spelman College

By the Numbers

General Information

Spelman College
350 Spelman Lane
Atlanta, GA 30314-4399

Control:
Private

Academic Calendar:
Semester

Religious Affiliation:
None

Founded:
1881

Web Site:
www.spelman.edu

Main Phone:
(404) 682-3643

Student Body

Full-Time Undergraduates:
2,221

Part-Time Undergraduates:
197

Total Male Undergraduates:
18

Total Female Undergraduates:
2,300

Admissions

Overall Acceptance Rate:
39%

Total Applicants:
4,534

Total Acceptances:
1,771

Freshman Enrollment:
531

Yield (% of admitted students who actually enroll):
32%

Early Decision Available?
Yes

Early Decision Notification:
December 15

Early Action Available?
Yes

Early Action Deadline:
November 15

Early Action Notification:
December 31

Regular Decision Deadline:
February 1

Regular Decision Notification:
April 1

Must-Reply-By Date:
May 1

Applicants Placed on Waiting List:
102

Applicants Accepting a Place on Waiting List:
43

Students Enrolled from Waiting List:
2

Transfer Applications Received:
263

Transfer Applications Accepted:
76

Transfer Students Enrolled:
47

Transfer Application Acceptance Rate:
29%

Common Application Accepted?
Yes

Supplemental Forms?
No

Admissions Phone:
(800) 982-2411

Admissions E-Mail:
admiss@spelman.edu

Admissions Web Site:
www.spelman.edu/students/prospective/getting_in

SAT I or ACT Required?
Either

**SAT I Range
(25th–75th Percentile):**
1010–1180

**SAT I Verbal Range
(25th–75th Percentile):**
510–600

**SAT I Math Range
(25th–75th Percentile):**
500–580

**ACT Composite Range
(25th–75th Percentile):**
21–25

Freshman Retention Rate:
90%

**Top 10% of
High School Class:**
33%

Application Fee:
$35

**Students Also Applied to
These Schools:**
Clark Atlanta University, Florida A&M University, Georgia Institute of Technology, Hampton University, Howard University

Financial Information

Tuition:
$17,005

Room and Board:
$8,750

Books and Supplies:
$1,700

**Average Need-Based
Financial Aid Package
(including loans, work-study,
grants, and other sources):**
$10,500

**Students Who Applied
for Financial Aid:**
92%

Students Who Received Aid:
82%

Financial Aid Forms Deadline:
March 1

Financial Aid Phone:
(404) 270-5212

Financial Aid E-Mail:
admiss@spelman.edu

Financial Aid Web Site:
www.spelman.edu/students/prospective/scholarships

Academics

The Lowdown On...
Academics

Degrees Awarded:
Bachelor of Arts
Bachelor of Science

Most Popular Majors:
28% Social Sciences
19% Psychology
13% Biological Sciences
11% English Language/ Literature
5% Visual and Performing Arts

Full-Time Faculty:
169

Faculty with Terminal Degree:
85%

Student-to-Faculty Ratio:
12:1

Class Sizes:
Fewer than 20 Students: 56%
20 to 49 Students: 42%
50 or more Students: 1%

Graduation Rates:
Four-Year: 62%
Five-Year: 73%
Six-Year: 74%

Special Degree Options
Dual Degree Engineering Program, independent major option

AP Test Score Requirements
Possible credit for scores of 3, 4, or 5

IB Test Score Requirements
Possible credit for scores of 3, 4, or 5

Best Places to Study
Study areas in the dorms, your dorm room, the library

Sample Academic Clubs
The Biology Club, the Economics Club, the French Club, National Society of Black Engineers, Pre-Law Society, the Psychology Club

Did You Know?

The 2005 edition of *U.S. News & World Report* ranked Spelman **among the Top 75 Best Liberal Arts Colleges**.

It is bad luck to walk through the Alumnae Arch located within the campus Oval before your senior class participates in the "March Through the Alumnae Arch."

Spelman is part of the Atlanta University Center, the largest consortium of Historically Black Colleges and Universities in the world. Spelman and five other schools (Clark Atlanta University, Morris Brown College, the Interdenominational Theological Center, Morehouse College, and the Morehouse School of Medicine) share cross-registration and the resources of the Robert W. Woodruff Library. Visit *www.aucenter.edu* for more info.

Spelman now has wireless Internet! Feel free to put the final touches on your writing assignment at the student center on your way from class!

Students Speak Out On...
Academics

> "The teachers are very approachable and really want you to succeed. They really go out of their way for you if you reach out to them. Classes are interesting, and discussions can be quite lively."

> "The professors in both the department of biology and department of philosophy were amazing. Not only had they all been published, **they all knew innovative ways to convey the information**, had the right questions to ask to spark further interest, and made themselves available to students outside of class."

> "In biology, the professors had lab assistants and would work with the students to enhance their learning while at Spelman. In philosophy, the professors held seminar style classes and gave assignments that made the students want to work, to question, to think, and to solidify or modify their own beliefs. Because of the small student-to-teacher ratio, **I was able to have good relationships with my professors**, which aided in my matriculation and overall experience at Spelman. Often, I would learn something in class and then gain an even deeper understanding in the professor's office hours."

> "It truly is a nurturing environment because of the class size. **The professor will know your name and will foster a relationship with you**. As far as classes, my first year I took freshman requirements, so they weren't as exciting as classes I selected for my major. ADW (African Diaspora and the World) was by far one of the most difficult classes to adjust to as an incoming freshman, yet it was one of the classes where I took the most knowledge from."

Q "I find that the teachers are, for the most part, very accommodating. **They are really concerned with your well-being far beyond the classroom**. They take into consideration your other involvements. I think they try to keep the class as structured as possible, but when it comes down to it, they want you to do the best you can. As a political science major, my classes are very interesting. The course requirements all fall within the subject matter, and assignments are good."

Q "I would say that **90 percent of my teachers were brilliant, warm, and caring**, and they were genuinely concerned about me as an individual."

Q "These instructors go above and beyond the call of duty to prepare you for real-world challenges. They understand and **educate you on the challenges of being a woman of color living the U.S.**, and in many ways, they over-prepare you for the real world, so you are not standing with other college graduates academically, you're standing above them. Our professors are also walking history books, and whether it is Dr. Christine King Farris (Dr. Martin Luther King's sister) or Dr. Marilyn Davis (political science professor), they can offer you so much perspective from how they lived, not just from what they have read."

Q "I was a computer science major, so I generally kept the same teachers from year to year, which was great in my opinion. Some of the classes were interesting, but I have to admit that **I took some classes based on the teacher because I knew that it would be an easy A**!"

Q "Overall, the teachers are great! They're enthusiastic about teaching, dedicated to academic advancement, and committed to their subject matter. **Teachers are very concerned about developing the 'whole woman.'**"

Q "I was a biology major, and I enjoyed my teachers quite a bit. The special thing about the professors at Spelman is that the teachers really care about you. **They notice when you aren't in class and call you on it**. They know about your life and your family, and by the time you graduate, many of them are family, too."

Q "I find the classes in my major to be interesting. Some of the other core classes that are outside the rest of my life don't really apply. **My teachers seem to be passionate, so they try to make it interesting**, and that counterbalances and keeps me motivated."

Q "Most of the teachers that I had while I matriculated at Spelman were very knowledgeable about their respective fields. They were interested not only in my academic development but in my development as a responsible adult who was civic-minded and connected to the community. **Many of the teachers had an old-fashioned approach to teaching**, and they would lock you out of class if you were late or throw you out of class if you were talking in the middle of a lecture, but their approach was one that I can now appreciate."

The College Prowler Take On...
Academics

Spelman places emphasis on the entire college experience, including academics. Classes are kept to small groups of students, allowing for easy interaction with peers and instructors. Almost every class is taught by a professor, and the College makes little use of TAs as instructors. Dialogue in the classroom is open, and it is common to find a discussion that has wandered away from the course syllabus to a relevant current event. One mandatory freshman course, African Diaspora & the World (ADW), inspires discussions about issues faced by those of African descent throughout history. Regardless of the class, most professors are approachable and sincerely interested in their students as people.

Spelman is academically sound, and not only because of its well-known and published professors or the recognition it receives in the press. At all levels students are challenged to take on both group and individual projects meant to expand their knowledge, as well as enhance their approach to problem solving. Spelman has always had a strong reputation as a liberal arts college. In recent years, the college has widened that reputation to include the sciences with the addition of the Albro Falconer Manley Science Center. There is a strong emphasis on studies and the pursuit of graduate degrees. Some instructors believe in conducting their classes and disciplining students in a traditional style that, by today's standards, may seem strict, but students will have a unique connection with professors.

The College Prowler® Grade on
Academics: B+

A high Academics grade generally indicates that professors are knowledgeable, accessible, and genuinely interested in their students' welfare. Other determining factors include class size, how well professors communicate, and whether or not classes are engaging.

Local Atmosphere

The Lowdown On...
Local Atmosphere

Region:
Southeast

City, State:
Atlanta, GA

Setting:
Large city

Distance from Charlotte:
4 hours and 30 minutes

Points of Interest:
Fernbank Museum
Georgia Aquarium
High Museum of Art
Martin Luther King Jr. National Historical Site
World of Coca-Cola
Zoo Atlanta

Movie Theaters:

XAMC Theatres Phipps
Plaza 14
3500 Peachtree Rd. NE
Atlanta

Cinefe: Cinema & Café:
2244 Panola Rd.
Lithonia

Landmark Midtown
Arts Cinemas
931 Monroe Dr. NE
Atlanta
(678) 495-1424

Magic Johnson Theatre
2841 Greenbriar Pkwy. SW
Atlanta
(404) 629-0000

Starlight Six Drive-In
2000 Moreland Ave. SE
Atlanta
(404) 627-5786

Shopping Malls:

17th St. shopping district
Cumberland Mall
East Atlanta Village
Greenbriar Mall
The Mall at West End
North Dekalb Mall
Phipps Plaza
Underground Atlanta

Major Sports Teams:

Atlanta Braves (Baseball)
Atlanta Falcons (Football)
Atlanta Hawks (Basketball)
Atlanta Thrashers (Hockey)

City Web Sites

www.atlantaga.gov

www.ajc.com

www.accessatlanta.com

Did You Know?

5 Fun Facts about Atlanta:
- Georgia is known as the Peach State, and **Atlanta is often referred to as "the ATL**," "Hot-Lanta," and "A-Town."
- **The 1995 Olympics were held in Atlanta**. As a result, Centennial Park was created. This is a nice area to visit in the summer and serves as the venue for many open-air concerts and festivals.
- Downtown Atlanta will be home to the new state-of-the-art Georgia Aquarium. **It will be the largest aquarium in the world**, with 8 million gallons of fresh and marine water.
- Restaurants have become the newest places to see and be seen in Atlanta. **With hundreds of spots that range from fine dining to burgers and fries**, you won't run out of options, but you'll have to watch your weight!
- Movies such *The Gospel*, *Diary of a Mad Black Woman*, *Gone With the Wind*, and *Remember the Titans* were shot in Atlanta. **Filmmaker Spike Lee shot much of *School Days* in and around the Atlanta University Center** and included many Spelman students in the film.

Famous People from Atlanta:

Ciara, Dakota Fanning, Gladys Knight, Jermaine Dupri, John Mayer, Julia Roberts, Bow Wow, Ludacris, Martin Luther King Jr., Maynard Jackson, Michael Vick, Outkast (Big Boi, Andre 3000), Ryan Seacrest, TI, Ted Turner, Usher

Local Slang:

Bounce – To leave

Coke – What Atlantans call any carbonated, brown, soft drink

Crunk – Southern term for energized, pumped, or excited

Shawty – The word "shorty" with a Southern drawl. You might hear this as you walk around the town from men trying to get your attention. Advice—keep on moving!

Students Speak Out On...
Local Atmosphere

"**Atlanta is a perfect city for going to college. The atmosphere depends on the area of the city you are in; there is something for everyone.**"

Q "For sports, there are major arenas, leagues, and constant activities. For arts, there are museums, festivals, theaters, galleries, and classes. For food, there are plenty of restaurants that will satisfy any taste bud. Shopping malls, delectable restaurants, and clubs are located throughout the area. **If you need a break from the city life, the suburbs offer great getaways**, with spas, retreat centers, and hotels."

Q "**The West End of Atlanta where Spelman is located isn't one of the nicest areas**, and students don't really hang out there. If you do venture out in the West End, it's for necessities like getting food or going to CVS. Spelman, of course, is part of the Atlanta University Center, so we're in walking distance of Morehouse, Clark Atlanta University, and ITC."

Q "Atlanta is a great town. There are lots of things going on at all times in Atlanta. **Atlanta is one place where you can really see upwardly-mobile African Americans**. It has a rich history of African American leadership."

Q "**Atlanta has a very vibrant party atmosphere** that will quickly encompass your life. Luckily, by sophomore year, you will realize that every party is basically the same, with the same people doing the same things, and you don't have to go to the club every time its doors open."

Q "I can't think of anything specifically to stay away from, but be mindful of the people you're around. **Atlanta has its share of con men**, and they don't mind talking you out of your stuff. Atlanta has a thriving urban entertainment industry, but anyone who says they're in the industry is not. Don't allow them to take advantage of you in any way. There's also a number of homeless people in Atlanta, and they will ask you, a broke college student, for some cash. Most of them are harmless and just want a meal or money for the shelter, but some of them will get over on you."

Q "**Atlanta is a black mecca in terms of education and opportunity**. It's also home to many historic sites, including the archives at the Auburn Avenue Library, the history center, and the national registry near the capital that holds documentation of births and deaths back through the days of slavery."

Q "**Atlanta is a very lively place**. With professional sports teams, concerts almost every week, fabulous shopping, and dozens of colleges and universities, students in Atlanta are guaranteed to have a fun-filled undergraduate experience. The Atlanta University Center, which is home to Spelman College, Morehouse College, Clark Atlanta University, and the Interdenominational Theological Center, has activities that will keep students entertained 24/7. However, students should take time to venture outside of the West End and visit such sites as the Martin Luther King Jr. National Historic Site, CNN, Fernbank Museum, and the World of Coca-Cola."

The College Prowler Take On...
Local Atmosphere

Atlanta, lovingly known as HotLanta, is one of the fastest growing cities in the South. Attending Spelman College provides an opportunity to experience the small community setting nestled within the gates, as well a chance to venture out and explore all that Atlanta has to offer. Spelman is just a short walk from MARTA, Atlanta's public transportation system. Hop on, and you will find some shopping malls and restaurants, but you will notice relatively quickly that, in this sprawling city, you really can't get around without a car.

Atlanta plays host to many conferences and festival events. The National Black Arts Festival, Music Midtown, and most recently the VIBE Music Festival are three of the events that help make Atlanta a cultural hub. With more movies being shot in the city, celebrity sightings are picking up. History is big in Atlanta, and you will see historical markers throughout the city commemorating everything form the Civil War to the Civil Rights Movement. You'll find the people in Atlanta to be friendly and inviting. Nothing beats Southern hospitality, and there is enough to go around in this town. Many people agree that "no one in Atlanta is from Atlanta." While Atlanta attracts many bright students, entrepreneurs and families, it also, like any large city, has a criminal element. Be careful, and watch out for con artists. When buying from street vendors in the city, a bargain may be easy to find, but the name brand on the bag may be covering up a fake.

The College Prowler® Grade on
Local Atmosphere: A-

A high Local Atmosphere grade indicates that the area surrounding campus is safe and scenic. Other factors include nearby attractions, proximity to other schools, and the town's attitude toward students.

Safety & Security

The Lowdown On...
Safety & Security

Number of Spelman Security Officers:
30

Spellman Campus Security Phone:
(404) 525-6401

Safety Services:
Adopt-A-Dorm
Fight Back
POSSE (Protecting Our Spelman Sisters Everyday)

Health Services:
Advice nurse
Clinical laboratory
Cold self-care station
Consultant services
Flu shots
Health education
Immunizations
Inhalation therapy
Nutrition counseling
Physical exams
Primary medical clinic
Sick-call clinic
Travel clinic
Women's health clinic

Health Center:
Student Health Services
Historic MacVicar Hall
350 Spelman Ln.
(404) 270-5249
Hours: Monday–Friday
9 a.m.–5 p.m. (fall/spring),
closed on weekends and
holidays

Did You Know?

Men are not allowed on Spelman's campus after visitation hours are over. This rule does not change after freshman year.

Students Speak Out On...
Safety & Security

"The guards were great, and we all knew what the rules were. Despite the few incidents that took place on campus, for the most part, I felt safe and secure behind the gates of Spelman College."

Q "Spelman's security is top-notch. **Sure, we complained about it, but darnit, it's pretty good**! If you were on campus, you were within the fortress walls."

Q "Spelman police **think they are the FBI**!"

Q "It is pretty good, I guess. I feel like the security guards are sort of a front. **I don't think that they really know what they are doing**. It is working because people are scared of them, but am I really safe if something did go down?"

Q "I felt very secure on campus, and I even feel like our Public Safety on campus tries to help us off campus. What I mean by that is they will be posted by the MARTA or down the street. **They also have self-defense classes to make sure we are prepared**."

Q "Every now and then an incident will occur, but I can't recall any incident in the past five years where a student was hurt or violated on Spelman's campus. On the same note, **things can be very hush-hush around Spelman**, so unless it was huge, or someone you know witnessed it, you may never know. Spelman's Public Safety does do an excellent job on educating students on safety issues on and around the campus during their first-year orientation week."

Q "Safety on the campus is present. Also, **many of the guards are very friendly and helpful**."

Q "It is handled well. The gate is protected. **I feel secure on campus**. There were times I had to stay overnight to finish an art piece, and I always felt safe."

Q "Security is great to me. You almost get a false sense of security when you are within the gates. With the visibility of Public Safety, you feel like nothing can happen to you. Spelman is doing a great job of making students secure. **You have to remember that when you step outside those gates, it's a different world**. If you take that comfort outside the gates, you are guaranteed trouble."

Q "I don't live on campus anymore. I think there is a difference in having a gate around the campus. The fact that it is there provides security. Freshman year, there were some strange men on campus and people jumping the gate. **They give you a whistle freshman year**, and you should blow it if you are in danger, but that isn't really efficient. I know people who have blown the whistle, and no one came."

Q "Spelman is guarded by the Spelman College Public Safety office. **Security is tight, and Spelman is gated**. Men can visit dorms and dorm rooms, but must be off campus by midnight. Spelman dorms lock after midnight, but Spelman women can come and go as they like."

Q "No one can get through the gates. Basically, **it's very strict for guys**. I have always felt safe on campus. From the moment we get there they tell us to never go anywhere alone. At the end of this year, there was crime going on in West End. Inside the gate we are taken care of, but outside the gates we are in a rough neighborhood."

Q "Security is good, but **staying in groups is the safest way to travel**."

Q "**The first thing you learn is the number to Public Safety: (404) 525-6401**. It made you feel like if you were in trouble—even outside the gates—help is only a call away."

Q "Spelman College's security is second to none. The security officers took a personal interest in making sure we had fun but safe experiences at college. **They told us they would recognize us by face**, learn our names, and become familiar with our patterns of leaving and coming onto campus. These things they did. While some students may have felt like security was too interested, they did make sure that we remained safe."

The College Prowler Take On...
Safety & Security

Spelman takes on-campus security very seriously. Spelman has set visitation hours in the dorms specifically for males. This decreases the likelihood of non-Spelman students wandering the grounds after hours. You have to have both a dorm key and a room key to get in after midnight. Violent crime on campus is next to nonexistent, and the most you might have to deal with in the dorms is someone taking your calculator out of the study hall.

At times, you will find yourself on the surrounding campuses of Morehouse, Morris Brown College, and Clark Atlanta University (CAU). All three of these schools have full-time security, but one thing to keep in mind when you are walking in the areas around campus is that Spelman security does not patrol these areas as often. You won't find too many campuses safer than Spelman College. For many years, the entire college has been surrounded by an iron gate, and the school has front and back gate entrances, both of which are monitored by security at all times. The back gate is generally only open during school hours. The front gate is always open, but vehicle traffic is closely monitored. You cannot get on campus without being checked for credentials by an officer. Of course, it is a little easier for women to get on campus, as they will assume you are a student.

The College Prowler® Grade on
Safety & Security: A+

A high grade in Safety & Security means that students generally feel safe, campus police are visible, blue-light phones and escort services are readily available, and safety precautions are not overly necessary.

Computers

The Lowdown On...
Computers

High-Speed Network?
Yes

Number of Labs:
Three open access labs and one honors student lab

Operating Systems:
Mac OS X
Solaris (UNIX)
Windows

Number of Computers:
550

Wireless Network?
Yes

24-Hour Labs:
The general lab and the Albro Falconer-Manley Science Center lab

Free or Discounted Software?
None

Charge to Print?
None

Students Speak Out On...
Computers

"The lab is a good option for students. The hours are reasonable. I would recommend bringing your own, since the dorms are wired for Ethernet."

Q "The computers at Spelman are numerous and well-kept. The major labs have techs that can help when problems occur and have up-to-date equipment. **Around final exams, the Spelman labs are packed**, but there are others in the AUC (within walking distance) to offset the labs at Spelman. If you can't bring your own, there will be plenty of computers available to you."

Q "The computer lab is usually crowded around midterms and the end of the semester when people are scrambling to get work done. I think it's best to have your own computer. **I just used the computer lab to print out large documents**."

Q "Bring a computer if you plan to live off campus. Computer labs can be crowded during the day. **There is plenty of room in the evening**, though, if you stay on campus."

Q "You should have your own computer, because around midterms and finals the computer lab gets pretty full. **A laptop may prove more beneficial than a PC** because you may need to get work done in the library or in other environments."

Q "The best part is that **there is no cost for paper**. You can use the computers freely."

Q "**The general computer lab is crowded depending on the time of day that you go** and also depending on the time of the semester (e.g., when papers or research projects are due). If you chose to bring your own computer, then Spelman also has an MIS staff (including student interns) that are available to help you if you have personal computer problems."

Q "**I would advise everyone who is able to bring their own computers to do so.** Twenty-four hour computer labs are on campus, but they tend to get crowded around midterms and finals. Plus, realistically speaking, you won't feel like walking to the computer lab at 2 a.m. when you finally decide to work on your paper or project."

The College Prowler Take On...
Computers

At Spelman there is a computer lab or cluster in almost every academic building. The best thing is that students can print out papers for free. Crowded computer labs are an issue more during the day than at night. If you live on campus, you might have more luck after hours finding an available station. If the computer labs on Spelman's campus are at capacity, the other Atlanta University Center schools have labs that are open to you. As with Spelman, students of the school where the lab resides have priority, but you will not be denied access if there is a station available. The general lab is open 24 hours, and all you need to get in is your student ID to swipe at the entrance.

If you don't want the hassle of waiting in a computer lab or you live off campus, you may want to bring a laptop or PC along. If you do bring your own computer and are not tech savvy, you will find that the student-staffed help desk will help you with any computer-related issues you may have. Spelman has come a long way in recent years with regard to computer facilities. Class registration, which used to be an all-day process of standing in line, is now a simple point-and-click process online. Instructors are making more use of online options as well. Liberal arts majors will probably find that the computer labs fit their needs, while techies may find the resources adequate but not overwhelmingly advanced in nature.

The College Prowler® Grade on
Computers: B

A high grade in Computers designates that computer labs are available, the computer network is easily accessible, and the campus's computing technology is up-to-date.

Facilities

The Lowdown On...
Facilities

Student Center:
Manley Student Center

Athletic Centers:
The Fitness Center

Campus Size:
50 acres

Libraries:
Robert W. Woodruff Library

Popular Places to Chill:
The Manley Student Center, The Student Center at Clark Atlanta University, Kilgore (the Morehouse Student Center), the "Strip" (a walkway on CAU's campus where people chill to see and be seen), and (believe it or not) the Woodruff Library, which is sometimes called "Club Woody."

What Is There to Do on Campus?

On Fridays, enjoy Market Friday at the student center. Take in a play put on by the drama majors at the fine arts theater. The gym has open hours to work out and classes to take. Visit the Spelman Museum of Fine Art to view the latest exhibit. Sisters Chapel is also on campus and will host many intellectual speakers throughout the year, as well as plays and concerts. Within the Atlanta University Center, King's Chapel and the Forbes Arena, both on the Morehouse campus, always host concerts, step shows, or parties that are worth the walk. The same is true of the Davage Auditorium on CAU's campus.

Movie Theater on Campus?

No

Bowling on Campus?

Yes, but only a couple of lanes in the gym.

Coffeehouse on Campus?

Yes

Favorite Things to Do on Campus?

Most students like to take a strut through Market Friday at the student center to buy bargain fashions, music, and accessories, or to catch up between classes. Homecoming, usually celebrated jointly between Morehouse and Spelman, is a well-awaited yearly event filled with fashion shows, coronation of the College queens, music concerts, and the infamous tailgate party in the adjoining student parking lots.

Students Speak Out On...
Facilities

"**All of the facilities on campus are nice and very accessible. The only downfall is that the gym is not as developed and accessible as it should be.**"

Q "**The athletic facility at Spelman is small but sufficient**. All of the sports teams work together and share the equipment. The folks that run the place have schedules posted to make it easy to know when there are openings. It has a basketball court, aerobics/yoga workout room, a gym, outdoor tennis courts, and a pool. There are always classes going on for pilates, yoga, and aerobics. There are teams that need to use other facilities in the city, like the golf team and soccer team."

Q "**The student center (Lower Manley) is the place to be to find out what events are going on**, to connect with friends, to meet up with visitors from other campuses, to play pool, and to get some good food. The indoor part of the center is on the floor under the cafeteria, and then there is an outside area where Market Friday is held. This is when local vendors come to offer their services and products. You can find everything like T-shirts, jewelry, shoes, sundresses, CDs, DVDs, food, and entertainment. Everyone in the AUC comes over and just has some fun to start the weekend off right."

Q "In recent years, campus buildings have been upgraded to remain competitive with larger universities; however, **the beauty lies in the fact that the new construction blends beautifully with the historic structures**, like Giles & Packard."

Q "Depending on the building you're in, the facilities are older, yet functional. The student center is evolving. It's not as large as other campuses', and it could have more things for students to do besides watching TV. The gym is really dated and small. **For a women's college that promotes healthy living, I'm surprised that there isn't a larger gym**. We go over to Morehouse to use their student center and gym. It's huge!"

Q "**The science center is nice**, and the student center is pretty nice, too."

Q "The facilities on campus are nice, and **the ones that aren't so nice are being updated**. Patience is a virtue."

Q "The facilities on campus are decent. **Some of the academic buildings are a little outdated**; however, Spelman is actively working to build new state-of-the-art facilities and renovate the other facilities."

The College Prowler Take On...
Facilities

On the campus of a college that was founded over 100 years ago, you should expect some older, smaller buildings, but the facilities on Spelman's campus are mixed when it comes to design and modern amenities. The Manley Student Center is home to the cafeteria and a social area, and most students find it a nice escape from the dormitory. Sisters Chapel recently had a much-needed facelift, and students and alumni are both pleased with the results. This facility has a great deal of history behind it and is home to most of the schools major presentations and entertainment events.

Students complain most about the gym, as it is relatively small and offers limited equipment. Some students still find that they have to join the local Bally's or LA Fitness in order to get the type of workout they need. Though Spelman's campus doesn't offer a great deal of variety when it comes to facilities and day-to-day activities, there are always events being put on that create a buzz on campus. Also, the proximity of the campus to other schools in the Atlanta University Center gives students the freedom to explore and enjoy facilities they like better elsewhere. Spelman is a work in progress, and students can expect that there will be more renovations to come to make the campus competitive with other schools.

The College Prowler® Grade on
Facilities: B-

A high Facilities grade indicates that the campus is aesthetically pleasing and well-maintained; facilities are state-of-the-art, and libraries are exceptional. Other determining factors include the quality of both athletic and student centers and an abundance of things to do on campus.

Campus Dining

The Lowdown On...
Campus Dining

Freshman Meal Plan Requirement?
Yes

Meal Plan Average Cost:
Included in tuition

Places to Grab a Bite with Your Meal Plan:

Jaguar Underground (AKA the Grill)
Food: Wings, sandwiches, smoothies and burgers
Location: Manley College Center
Hours: Monday–Thursday 8:30 a.m.–10:30 a.m., Friday 8:30 a.m.–4 p.m., Sunday 5:30 p.m.–10:30 p.m.

Alma Upshaw Dining Hall

Food: Hot entrees, pizza, sandwiches, salads

Location: Manley College Center

Hours: Monday–Friday 7 a.m.–10 a.m., 11:30 a.m.–2 p.m., 4:30 p.m.–6:30 p.m., Saturday–Sunday 7:30 a.m.–10 a.m., 11 a.m.–2 p.m., 4:30 p.m.–6 p.m.

Off-Campus Places to Use Your Meal Plan:

None

24-Hour Dining:

No, but each dorm has vending machines with snacks.

Did You Know?

At one time, **students from other schools would sneak into the Spelman cafeteria to eat** because it had the best food in the Atlanta University Center!

Students Speak Out On...
Campus Dining

"Dining on campus is pretty good. When I get tired of the dining hall, we have fresh deli sandwiches on campus. If I get tired of that, I can always walk to the surrounding restaurants."

Q "Food on campus is great whenever parents or prospective students are there. On a daily basis, though, it's okay. **We always get excited about fried chicken Wednesdays and catfish Fridays**, but other than that, it's just your everyday cafeteria food."

Q "The cafeteria is good. **We finally got vegan and vegetarian accommodations**. There are daily options like pizza, subs, waffles, and pasta, and there are special options occasionally, depending on events and holidays. It's important to remember that it is a cafeteria, not a restaurant—then you won't be disappointed."

Q "The main dining hall food is not above par, but it is decent. **I personally would go to the caf to eat**, but if I had money, I would go to the Grill. You can hang out there and watch TV."

Q "The cafeteria sucks. We have good days. Wednesday is fried chicken day, and it is crowded so get there early. In addition to the cafeteria menu, a woman makes fresh pasta to order and another prepares vegetarian. You can specify what you want in the order; for example, 'no onions.' **The pasta line and vegetarian line won't let you down**."

Q "**Breakfast, lunch, and dinner are provided**, and there are selections for everyone, like vegetarian and vegan options."

Q "I haven't eaten in the caf since my freshman year. It doesn't look very good. **The Grill is good, it's just kind of overpriced**."

Q "**Two days: fried chicken day (Wednesday) and fried fish friday**! Those are the good days, as well as brunch on Sundays. The other days are a struggle. We only have two places where you can eat—the cafeteria or downstairs. The venue for downstairs always changes, and it's more expensive. Also, both spots tend to close pretty early, so if you're hungry past, like, 6:30, you're out of luck. A lot of people tend to order out."

Q "**There is one main dining hall**, and the best items are the cereal, the cake, and the pasta."

Q "Food on campus is really not that great. There is one dining hall and one grill/fast food place. **The food could really use improvement**."

Q "As a very picky eater, I never ate in the cafeteria. When I was desperate, **I took a 15-minute walk to Wendy's in the West End** and stopped at Krispy Kreme on the trek back to campus."

Q "Food in the cafeteria is basic cafeteria food. If you are hungry, you eat it. If I had a choice, and the Grill was free like the cafeteria, I would go there. It isn't like other schools. **The Grill is where it's at, but the food is sometimes a little bland**. I like to grab a smoothie and keep it moving."

Q "**I don't care for the dining hall**. It seems like they just throw everything together."

Q "They are making improvements. **I stay off campus, but they have things for vegans and vegetarians**. When they have fried chicken Wednesday, they offer baked chicken, too."

Q "The food on campus leaves much to be desired. Breakfast is pretty good. They have a wide variety. Lunch is pretty consistent. **You know you are guaranteed hot dogs and hamburgers Tuesday and Thursday**. Dinner is horrible, and it is almost like they say 'the faculty is gone now, so let's just put something out here.' The food is okay. The Grill is good, but it is a little overpriced and portions aren't great. It's fast food."

Q "I personally think the dining hall is edible. The problem I have is the workers are stingy. **It is supposed to be all you can eat, but none of it is self-serve**. If you ask for extra, they tell you to come back. That bothers me. They have the salad bar, pasta, hot meals, sandwiches, and anything you could want. I think it is good that they cater to the vegetarian crowd. The thing with the Grill, so you don't have to walk around with cash, is that you can add money to your ID. You start out with $25."

Q "As far as the main dining hall, I never really ate there much, except for freshman year because I was forced to live on campus. **The dining hall is okay, but the Grill is better**. They serve hamburgers. More people eat there than in the actual cafeteria. They have wings, smoothies, and those types of things."

The College Prowler Take On...
Campus Dining

Spelman only offers two choices when it comes to dining. You can either go upstairs to the cafeteria or go downstairs for somewhat of a fast food experience. Many students agree that the food is just mediocre. The hours that you can eat are also rigid. You cannot find hot food on campus 24 hours a day. In fact, there is no such thing as a late dinner in the campus cafeteria either. Dinner ends at 6:30 p.m., and if you don't get in by then, you can go downstairs and grab something to eat at the the Jaguar Underground (the "Grill"). The weekends are the worst. The downstairs option is not available on Saturday, so you are forced to eat in the cafeteria. Within the dorms, you will find that you can microwave meals and prepare quick items; however, you cannot have refrigerators or cooking devices inside your actual room.

The good thing about the Spelman meal plan is that it is included in your tuition, and your ID card gives you access and is preloaded with $25 for the the Grill. After that, you have to stock up the card on your own. It seems like the highlights of the week for most students are fried fish Friday, fried chicken Wednesday, and the Spelman Sunday brunch. Other than that, students don't have much to say about eating on campus. It is safe to say that perhaps this is not one of the strong points of the College.

The College Prowler® Grade on
Campus Dining: C

The grade on Campus Dining addresses the quality of both school-owned dining halls and independent on-campus restaurants as well as the price, availability, and variety of food.

Off-Campus Dining

The Lowdown On...
Off-Campus Dining

Restaurant Prowler: Popular Places to Eat!

Beautiful Restaurant
Food: Soul food
2284 Cascade Rd., Cascade
(404) 758-4000
Price: $5–$10 per person
Hours: Sunday–Tuesday 12 p.m.–9 p.m., Wednesday–Saturday 11 a.m.–9 p.m.

Benihana
Food: Japanese steakhouse
229 Peachtree St., Downtown
(404) 425-9629
Cool Features: Cooks put on a show at your table!
Price: $12–$20 per person
Hours: Monday–Thursday 11 a.m.–1:45 p.m., 5 p.m.–9:30 p.m., Friday 11 a.m.–1:45 p.m., 5 p.m.–10:30 p.m., Saturday 5 p.m.–10:30 p.m., Sunday 1:30 p.m.–9 p.m.

Big Daddy's
Food: Soul food
Corner of Luckie & Forsyth St., Downtown
(404) 659-1756
Price: $8–$15 person
Hours: Daily 24 hours

Busy Bee Café
Food: Soul food
810 Martin Luther King Jr. Dr. SW, West End
(404) 525-9212
Cool Features: If you've never had chittlins, ox tails, or neck bones, get a taste here.
Price: $7–$10 per person
Hours: Monday–Friday
11 a.m.–7 p.m.,
Sunday 12 p.m.–7 p.m.

Café Intermezzo
Food: Coffeehouse, desserts
1845 Peachtree St., Midtown
(404) 223-3202
Price: $10–$15 per person
Hours: Monday–Thursday
11 a.m.–3 a.m.,
Friday 11 a.m.–4 a.m.,
Saturday 10:30 a.m.–4 a.m.,
Sunday 10:30 a.m.–3 a.m.

The Cheesecake Factory
Food: American
3024 Peachtree Rd., Buckhead
(404) 816-2555
Cool Features: Over 30 varieties of cheesecake

(The Cheesecake Factory, continued)
Price: $10–$20 per person
Hours: Monday–Thursday
11:30 a.m.–11 p.m.,
Friday–Saturday
11:30 a.m.–12:30 a.m.,
Sunday 10 a.m.–11 p.m.

City Café
Food: Diner
525 10th St., Midtown
(404) 724-5713
Price: $8–$12 per person
Hours: Daily 24 hours

Egg Roll Corner
Food: Chinese
825 Martin Luther King Jr. Dr.
(404) 526-9099
Cool Features: You can walk here in 15 minutes from Spelman's back gate.
Price: $5–$10 per person
Hours: Sunday–Thursday
11 a.m.–10 p.m., Friday–Saturday 11 a.m.–11 p.m.

Fellini's Pizza
Food: Pizza, Italian
909 Ponce de Leon Ave.
(404) 873-3088
Cool Features: They have a large outdoor patio.
Price: $5–$8 per person
Hours: Monday–Saturday
11:30 a.m.–2 a.m.,
Sunday 12 p.m.–12 a.m.

Gladys & Ron's Chicken & Waffles
Food: Breakfast, soul food
529 Peachtree Rd., Midtown
(404) 874-9393
Cool Features: Gladys Knight and Ron Winans co-own it.
Price: $10–$15 per person
Hours: Monday–Thursday 11 a.m.–11 p.m., Friday–Saturday 11 a.m.–4 a.m. Sunday 11 a.m.–8 p.m.

Gordon Biersch Brewery
Food: American
848 Peachtree St. NE, Midtown
(404) 870-0805
Cool Features: On-site beer brewing!
Price: $10–$20 per person
Hours: Monday–Thursday 11:30 a.m.–12 a.m., Friday–Saturday 11:30 a.m.–2 a.m.

Houston's
Food: American
3321 Lenox Rd., Buckhead
(404) 237-7534
Price: $15–$30 per person
Hours: Monday–Saturday 11 a.m.–11 p.m., Sunday 11 a.m.–10:30 p.m.

La Fonda Latina
Food: Cuban, Latin American
923 Ponce De Leon Ave., Midtown
(404) 607-4211

(La Fonda Latina, continued)
Cool Features: Sangria and sopa de pollo
Price: $8–$12 per person
Hours: Monday–Thursday 11:30 a.m.–11 p.m., Friday–Saturday 11:30 a.m.–12 a.m., Sunday 12:30 p.m.–11 p.m.

Landmark Diner
Food: Coffee, sandwiches
3652 Roswell Rd.
(404) 816-9090
Price: $5–$10 per person
Hours: Daily 24 hours

Maggiano's
Food: Italian
3368 Peachtree Rd., Buckhead
(404) 816-9650
Price: $15–$25 per person
Hours: Sunday–Thursday 11 a.m.–10 p.m., Friday–Saturday 11 a.m.–12 a.m.

Noche
Food: Southwestern tapas
1000 Virginia Ave., Virginia Highlands
(404) 815-9155
Cool Features: Voted "best margarita" by *Jezebel* magazine.
Price: $8–$15 per person
Hours: Sunday–Thursday 5 p.m.–10 p.m., Friday 5 p.m.–11 p.m., Saturday 1 p.m.–11 p.m., Sunday 1 p.m.–10 p.m.

Pappadeaux Seafood Kitchen
Food: Cajun seafood
2830 Windy Hill Rd., Marietta
(770) 984-8899
Cool Features: Fried alligator bites
Price: $10–$20 per person
Hours: Sunday–Thursday 11 a.m.–10 p.m., Friday–Saturday 11 a.m.–11 p.m.

Pappasito's
Food: Mexican
2788 Windy Hill Rd., Marietta
(770) 541-6100
Price: $10–$20 per person
Hours: Sunday–Thursday 11 a.m.–10 p.m., Friday–Saturday 11 a.m.–11 p.m.

Paschal's
Food: Soul food
180 Northside Dr., West End
(404) 525-2023
Price: $10–$20 per person
Hours: Monday–Thursday 11 a.m.–10 p.m., Friday–Saturday 11 a.m.–11 p.m., Sunday 11 a.m.–9 p.m.

R. Thomas Deluxe Grill
Food: Healthy American
1812 Peachtree St., Midtown
(404) 872-2942
Cool Features: All organic
Price: $8–$15 per person
Hours: Daily 24 hours

Red Lobster
Food: Seafood
2522 Candler Rd., Decatur
(404) 243-4121
Cool Features: Shrimp Feast!
Price: $8–$15 per person
Hours: Sunday–Thursday 11 a.m.–10 p.m., Friday–Saturday 11 a.m.–11 p.m.

RuSan's
Food: Sushi, Japanese
1529 Piedmont Rd., Midtown
(404) 875-7042
Cool Features: Cheap, tasty sushi. Good for those who are new to sushi.
Price: $8–$10 per person
Hours: Monday–Friday 4:30 p.m.–12 a.m.

Savage Pizza
Food: Pizza, Italian
484 Moreland Ave., East Atlanta
(404) 523-0500
Cool Features: Great calzones
Price: $5–$10 per person
Hours: Monday–Thursday 11:30 a.m.–10:30 p.m., Friday–Saturday 11:30 a.m.–11:30 p.m., Sunday 12 p.m.–10:30 p.m.

Slice
Food: Italian
259 Peters St., West End
(404) 588-1820
Cool Features: A DJ spins on certain nights of the week.
Price: $5–$10 per person
Hours: Monday–Thursday
11 a.m.–12 a.m.,
Friday 11 a.m.–3 a.m.,
Saturday 12 p.m.–3 a.m.,
Sunday 12 p.m.–12 a.m.

Soul Vegetarian
Food: Healthy, soul food
652 N. Highland Ave., Virginia Highlands
(404) 875-4641
Cool Features: Soy shakes
Price: $10–$15 per person
Hours: Tuesday–Sunday
11 a.m.–10 p.m.

Taco Cabana
Food: Mexican
1895 Piedmont Ave., Midtown
(404) 874-6152
Cool Features: 99-cent margaritas on Friday
Price: $5–$10 per person
Hours: Daily 24 hours

The Tavern
Food: Traditional American
3500 Peachtree Rd., Buckhead
(404) 814-9640
Cool Features: Bartenders will put on a show.
Price: $15–$25 per person
Hours: Monday–Thursday
11 a.m.–11 p.m., Friday–Saturday 11 a.m.–12 a.m.,
Sunday 11 a.m.–10 p.m.

Waffle House
Food: Waffles, breakfast
3016 Piedmont Rd., Buckhead
(404) 231-0023
Cool Features: Near the club district
Price: $5–$10 per person
Hours: Daily 24 hours

Wing Zone
Food: Wings
710 Marietta St., Downtown
(404) 525-9464
Price: $5–$10 per person
Hours: Daily 4 p.m.–2 a.m.

Other Places to Check Out:
Applebee's
Beautiful Restaurant
Burger King
Chantrelle Restaurant
Church's Chicken
Popeye's Chicken
Starbucks
Wendy's

Student Favorites:
Busy Bee Café
Slice
Fellini's Pizza
The Cheesecake Factory

Grocery Stores:
Kroger
590 Cascade Rd.
(404) 756-1140

Publix
825 Martin Luther King Jr. Dr., West End
(404) 688-0174

24-Hour Dining:
City Café
Landmark Diner
R. Thomas Deluxe Grill
Taco Cabana
Waffle House

Best Breakfast:
Waffle House

Best Chinese:
Egg Roll Corner

Best Healthy:
R. Thomas Deluxe Grill
Soul Vegetarian

Best Pizza:
Slice
Fillini's Pizza

Best Wings:
Wing Zone

Best Place to Take Your Parents:
The Cheesecake Factory
The Tavern
Houston's
Pappadeaux

Did You Know?

Atlanta has started an annual Taste of Atlanta Festival in the Summer which provides attendees the chance to sample food from restaurants across the city. There is also the Downtown Restaurant Week which is done annually and lets you hop from place to place each evening enjoying a discount sampling of the best food the restaurants have to offer.

Students Speak Out On...
Off-Campus Dining

"There are so many restaurants in Atlanta. There is RuSan's, Houston's, and Benihana. We go to TGI Friday's a lot. Gladys & Ron's is good."

Q "Atlanta has some great options for dining on any budget. There is a Caribbean food place, Popeye's, Church's, Soul Vegetarian, the famous Paschal's, Burger King, and Wendy's within walking distance of the campus. Further into the city, there are all the big names like Cheesecake Factory, Maggiano's, TGI Friday's, and Applebee's. There are also some upscale spots for fine dining. Other places include R. Thomas', La Fonda (Cuban), and Savage Pizza. **You will definitely be able to find great food in the area**."

Q "**Atlanta has some great spots, as well as 'holes in the wall**.' City Café is 24 hours, and it's a great place to eat for college students, since it's only a couple of miles from Spelman. If you hop on the train and go to Buckhead, there are so many places to choose from. My personal favorite is the Cheesecake Factory."

Q "**Off campus, I like to eat late at night** at Landmark Diner. There is City Café on 10th Street and Northside. A lot of GA Tech students go there. Pappasito's is good. I enjoy pizza places like Fellini's and Slice by school."

Q "**Good spots are Chantrelle's, the Beautiful**, R. Thomas', Pappadeaux Seafood, and Intermezzo."

Q "**A good, cheap sushi place** people go to is RuSan's in midtown."

Q "There are many restaurants in Atlanta to choose from. **Some close spots to campus are Big Daddy's and the Busy Bee (both soul food)**."

Q "Slice is nice. It is five minutes from the school in an artsy area. **Big Daddy's is in Cascade and has good soul food**. Sometimes I used to go to the Morehouse caf, and they just recently built a coffeeshop over there."

Q "I like Gordon Biersch—the atmosphere and the place. **It is close to school and other places**. Starbucks is my favorite, especially the one on Peachtree across from Gordon Biersch."

Q "I love dining out. **Fellini's is one of my favorites, as well as another pizza place called Slice**. I also love Red Lobster."

The College Prowler Take On...
Off-Campus Dining

Dining off campus seems to be the way to go for many Spelman women. With dining halls offering limited choices and hours, students generally choose to make the voyage to their favorite restaurants. There seem to be quite a few places to get a quick bite to eat near the campus, but for sit-down dining, students have to go farther away from campus. Soul food is a general favorite among the student body, and there is no shortage of places to find it in Atlanta. Students also seem to gravitate toward pizza joints. Almost every student mentioned Slice or Fellini's as the best place to pick up a snack at almost all hours of the day and night. For students who want a little more menu variety after midnight, City Café, Landmark Diner, and R. Thomas are all open 24 hours a day.

Atlanta provides a wide variety of restaurants with entrees that are sure to please even the most discriminating taste buds. The biggest issue for students would be finding the transportation to get there. It would probably be helpful if there were more options closer to campus. However, students, led primarily by a craving for better tasting food, use public transportation and cars to get to a place that is more pleasing than what they would find on campus. From the most daring of diners to the most discriminating, Atlanta has room at the table for everyone.

The College Prowler® Grade on
Off-Campus Dining: A

A high Off-Campus Dining grade implies that off-campus restaurants are affordable, accessible, and worth visiting. Other factors include the variety of cuisine and the availability of alternative options (vegetarian, vegan, Kosher).

Campus Housing

The Lowdown On...
Campus Housing

Undergrads Living on Campus:
62%

Number of Dormitories:
10

Number of University-Owned Apartments:
2, Villages at Castleberry and Ashley Terrace (off campus)

Best Dorms:
LLC II
Morehouse James

Worst Dorms:
Abby
Manley

Freshmen Required to Live on Campus?
Yes

Dormitories:

Abby Aldrich Rockefeller Hall (Abby)
Floors: 3 + basement
Total Occupancy: 126
Bathrooms: Shared by floor
Residents: First-years
Room Types: Singles, doubles, triples, quads
Special Features: Computer lounge, exercise room, laundry facilities, vending areas, storage rooms, hall kitchens with microwaves

Bessie Strong Hall (Bessie Strong)
Floors: 2
Total Occupancy: 10
Bathrooms: Shared by floor
Residents: Upperclasswomen
Room Types: Singles
Special Features: Exercise room, key-card entry, kitchen, meditation rooms, meeting rooms, study/television lounges

Howard Harreld Hall (HH)
Floors: 3 + basement
Total Occupancy: 181
Bathrooms: Shared by floor
Residents: First-years
Room Types: Singles, doubles, triples, quads
Special Features: Aerobic facility, full kitchen, laundry facilities, vending areas, storage rooms

Dorothy Shepard Manley Hall (Manley)
Floors: 3 + basement
Total Occupancy: 131
Bathrooms: Shared by hall
Residents: First-years
Room Types: Singles, doubles, triples, quads
Special Features: Full kitchen with microwave, storage room, study lounge

Laura Spelman Residence Hall (Laura Spelman)
Floors: 3
Total Occupancy: 39
Bathrooms: Shared by floor
Residents: Upperclasswomen
Room Types: Singles, doubles
Special Features: Full kitchen, laundry facilities, study lounges

Living-Learning Center I (LLCI)
Floors: 3
Total Occupancy: 200
Bathrooms: Shared by floor
Residents: First-years and upperclasswomen, some honors students
Room Types: Singles, doubles
Special Features: Air-conditioning, conference rooms, courtyard, elevator, guest suites, hall kitchens with microwave, storage room, study lounges

Living-Learning Center II (LLCII)

Floors: 3
Total Occupancy: 200
Bathrooms: Shared by floor
Residents: First-years and upperclasswomen
Room Types: Singles, doubles
Special Features: Air-conditioning, auditorium, elevator, game rooms, laundry facilities, multifunctional gathering rooms, office of residential life, storage rooms

MacVicar Residence Hall

Floors: 2
Total Occupancy: 8
Bathrooms: Shared by floor
Residents: First-years and upperclasswomen
Room Types: Singles
Special Features: Hardwood floors, key-card entry, study/meeting rooms, vending area

Morehouse James Hall

Floors: 3 + basement
Total Occupancy: 84
Bathrooms: Shared by hall
Residents: Upperclasswomen
Room Types: Singles, doubles
Special Features: Commuter student computer lounge, laundry facilities, vending area

Sally Sage McAlpin Hall (McAlpin)

Floors: 3 + basement
Total Occupancy: 116
Bathrooms: Shared by hall
Residents: Upperclasswomen
Room Types: Singles, doubles
Special Features: Elevator, kitchenettes with stoves/microwaves, laundry facilities, study/television lounges, vending area

Housing Offered:

Singles: 30%
Doubles: 59%
Triples/Suites: 6%
Apartments: 3%
Other: 2%

Room Types

Residence halls include single-, double-, triple-, and quad-occupancy rooms. In all dorms, the majority of students share a central bathroom facility on each hall.

Apartments are located at two complexes off campus. One, Ashley Terrace Apartments, is for the sole use of the College, and the other, the Villages at Castleberry, is a mixed community of College and non-College residents. These units have full kitchens.

Bed Type

Standard twin

Cleaning Service

Each residence hall has housekeepers to regularly clean bathrooms showers and other public areas. Residents should clean up after gatherings and should assist in keeping common areas tidy.

What You Get

Bed, desk, chair, closet, dresser, local telephone service, high-speed Internet connection/Ethernet port, cable port, smoke-free living environment, vending services.

Also Available

Students in need of special accommodations can reach out to the Office of Disability Services at (404) 270-5289.

Did You Know?

Chadwick Hall, acquired in 1945, once stood in the space where the science center is now located. **This was originally the location of the Leonard Street Orphans home** and was converted to a dorm for usage by the school. The building was demolished in 1987.

Students Speak Out On...
Campus Housing

> "Dorm life is great. It is one of the most fun experiences you get when you first get to Spelman. It fosters the sense of sisterhood. The freshman dorms are like sororities."

Q "**The memories are more important** than the dorm you choose."

Q "I enjoyed staying in the dorm for three years. HH is the liveliest freshman dorm, while LLCI and LLCII are the more calm ones. **Don't come expecting a five-star hotel**, but the dorms at Spelman are definitely nice compared to other schools I have visited. Dorm life is a great way to meet people, stay up-to-date on activities and campus news, and is usually safer than off-campus housing because of the gate and security officers on post."

Q "Stay clear of McAlpin because the rooms are tiny. They have single rooms, but **you feel like you are in a closet**."

Q "The dorm rooms are **mostly small, and most have no air conditioning**. LLCI and LLCII have air, but the rooms are still small."

Q "I'm not going to list dorms to avoid, but **the dorm that I hold dear to my heart is Abby**—Abby Psi Phi till I die! I wouldn't have wanted to live anywhere else on campus."

Q "**Just bring a fan and Lysol**. Those are the top two things to have at school outside of books and pens."

Q "Of course you have your 'no air' issue, but we all come to Spelman expecting that. The dorm rooms are extremely small everywhere, so it is hard to feel at home when you feel like you are in a closet. They do their best to make you feel like you are in a family environment. **I suggest LLCI and LLCII because they are air-conditioned**. In the older dorms, like Morehouse James, the rooms are bigger. You have to decide what to sacrifice, space or air."

Q "The dorms are livable. Freshman year I stayed in the oldest dorm on campus, Howard Harreld Hall. **The dorm does not have air conditioning**; however, the living experience was very fun. Living Learning Centers I and II are very nice to live in as well. They have elevators, as well as computer labs and air conditioning; however, it is very hard to get into these dorms."

Q "**Best place to live freshman year is HH**, because it is the biggest dorm and you meet more people."

Q "**Unfortunately, a majority of the dorms are not air-conditioned**. While this may sound bad, with a couple fans you'll survive and have some interesting stories to share. You will be sharing the bathrooms with a number of girls, so shower shoes, Clorox wipes, and other sanitary products will be necessary. These bathrooms are cleaned daily, Monday through Friday, but not over the weekends—so best of luck from Friday evening until Monday afternoon. You'll need it."

Q "I lived on the third floor in Abby in one of the rooms with three beds. **It was small and cramped, but I loved it just the same**!"

Q "For incoming freshmen who are in the honors program, accommodations are pleasant, with air-conditioned dorms. For other incoming freshmen, **the charm of century-old buildings will have to suffice**."

Q "I don't stay on campus because I am from Atlanta. When I was able to stay in a few of them, **LLCII was the best one that I was able to stay in**. It is more advanced."

Q "Most buildings have a ground floor or basement floor. **Try not to stay on the ground floor, because they have the most bugs**."

The College Prowler Take On...
Campus Housing

For first-year students at Spelman, living on campus is mandatory. The best dorm for you will depend on your personality. For example, if you prefer the luxuries of hotel living, elevators, atriums, computer labs, and courtyards, your best bet is LLCI. This dorm is the newest and nicest of the first-year dorms. It is also home to upperclasswomen, and certain rooms are reserved for honors program members or scholarship recipients. Another option is Howard Harreld Hall, mostly referred to as HH. The camaraderie in this dorm is evident, it being the largest freshman dorm. Abby Hall is probably located the furthest from the front gates of Spelman, and, like HH, it offers singles through quads. It is sure to be a memorable experience for anyone with more than one roommate! Manley is one of the dorms that people just don't talk about much. By design, it is set up much like HH and is in proximity to the major buildings on campus.

Only certain dorms (LLCI and LLCII) are air-conditioned, and the ones that are seem to have the smallest rooms. Most students believe it is a choice between being hot or being confined. Front doors are locked in each dorm late at night and visitation, specifically male guests, is only allowed during certain hours. Overall, living conditions on campus are decent. The dorms are very conducive to studying and provide a safe and quiet environment.

The College Prowler® Grade on Campus Housing: B-

A high Campus Housing grade indicates that dorms are clean, well-maintained, and spacious. Other determining factors include variety of dorms, proximity to classes, and social atmosphere.

Off-Campus Housing

The Lowdown On...
Off-Campus Housing

Undergrads in Off-Campus Housing:
38%

Average Rent For:
Studio: $700 per month
1BR Apt.: $800 per month
2BR Apt.: $1,200 per month

Best Time to Look For a Place:
Spring semester or over the summer

Popular Areas:
Ashley Terrace Apartments
Buckhead
Cumberland
Midtown
Villages at Castleberry
West End

For Assistance Contact:
Office of International/Commuter Students
(404) 681-3643 Ext. 5143

Students Speak Out On...
Off-Campus Housing

"There are very convenient options like the Village at Castleberry. If you have a car, it's definitely worth it."

Q "Living off campus is definitely worth it! Once you've had your freshman (or sophomore) experience, it's time to move on! I think it's important to stay on campus for two years simply because it's best to foster friendships on campus. **Once you've established your friends, you can move off**. There are so many apartment complexes that are located near the MARTA if you don't have a car."

Q "If you don't have a strong friend base, it can be isolating moving off, and you tend to not know what's going on at campus sometimes, but there is always somebody who lives on campus that you know who can tell you where the parties are for the weekend or what events are going on at campus. **Overall, you save money when you're off of the meal plan and share rent with roommates**. And the important thing is you have privacy. No more communal bathrooms and people being aware of your comings and goings."

Q "**Atlanta has apartments, condos, and houses all at various price ranges**. I enjoyed renting a house with a couple of friends my senior year. If you are not a morning person, but have morning classes, I would suggest getting a place close to campus."

Q "Living off campus after freshman year is worth it to have your own kitchen and bathroom. **Plus, you can have men spend the night**."

Q "I moved off campus after my freshman year into the apartments across the street from Morris Brown (Northside Apartments). **It gave me freedom that the dorm didn't allow me** to have, but I also had a roommate to ease the pain of rent."

Q "Spelman has two apartment complexes, Ashley Terrace and Castleberry, that you can get through the school. **At Ashley Terrace you still have a RD**. Supposedly, the same visitation rules apply. Being an actual apartment complex makes it harder to monitor. It is nice because it's up the street. It has a shuttle to the campus, but it's not reliable. You still have that safe feel because it is only for Spelman students. Castleberry is nice, and is also a general property with other residents, but it is very close."

Q "Off-campus housing can be found with searching, and it's worth it if you live nearby. **Austell, Lithia Springs, and West End are all good areas to live**. Check *craigslist.org*, in the Atlanta Journal Constitution, and in the housing booklet on campus."

Q "Off-campus housing is pretty convenient after freshman year if you have a car. They have built apartments closer to campus, which is great. **One thing to keep in mind when moving off campus is Atlanta traffic**. It can be ridiculous, and it can turn a 15-minute drive into a 45-minute ordeal."

Q "My advice is this—don't do it unless you absolutely have to. Thinking about things for the moment, it seems like living off campus is great. You're on your own, ya know? A real grown-up. But looking at the bigger picture, you'll definitely save money by living on campus. It's convenient. Everything is right there, and **with gas prices the way they are, living on campus is much better**."

Q "Off-campus life is excellent! **I love living by myself**. There is nothing better. You get the freedom you want. If it is 11 p.m. and nothing is going on, you can invite everyone over. We live off Peachtree Street. We can walk to a club. It is worth it just for the experience. I think everyone should have that, because you grow up."

Q "Well, I think off campus is convenient. There is student living well within the region. It is definitely worth it because of the reduced cost and the freedom it provides. You have the ability to have guests come over at any time. With the rise in gas prices, it is something to think about having to make the commute everyday. **The only drawback is the commute**."

Q "**There are very convenient options like the Village at Castleberry**. If you have a car, it's definitely worth it."

Q "I stayed on campus my sophomore year, too. I have mixed feelings. **I feel like it is convenient to live on campus**. The further out you go, it is cheaper. A lot of people who drive 20 minutes to school say it takes away from the experience. If you only come to campus for class, you may not know about events. As long as it isn't too far, it is good, but the further you go away, the more it takes away from the experience."

The College Prowler Take On...
Off-Campus Housing

Living off campus is an excellent option for students after their first year. Spelman cannot guarantee housing for upperclasswomen, so it helps when a certain percentage take the plunge and move off the grounds. As with restaurants, there are living accommodations in Atlanta to fit all tastes. There are loft-style apartments for one, two, and three people, two-bedroom townhouses, homes for rent, and boarding houses within walking distance of the school or a short drive away. Many students believe that living off campus saves money, though this can be debated. Some students live in posh downtown apartments, and when you add rent, utilities, gas, entertainment, and dining, you might find you are spending more. There is something to be said, however, for the freedom and responsibility you gain once off campus.

Start your search early, as some of the more popular apartment complexes may have a waiting list. You have to make an extra effort once you are off campus to stay plugged in to the day-to-day activities, since, if you only have classes on Tuesdays and Thursdays, the connection you have as a Spelmanite may start to fade. On the positive side, this will give you a chance to explore all that Atlanta has to offer. Balance is the key to a healthy and productive living situation while at Spelman. If you can achieve that off campus, then you should go for it.

The College Prowler® Grade on
Off-Campus Housing: A+

A high grade in Off-Campus Housing indicates that apartments are of high quality, close to campus, affordable, and easy to secure.

Diversity

The Lowdown On...
Diversity

African American:
95%

Native American:
Less than 1%

Asian American:
Less than 1%

White:
3%

Hispanic:
Less than 1%

Unknown:
0%

International:
2%

Out-of-State:
71%

Political Activity

Most students are politically and socially liberal. Ask any alumnae from the '60s, and they will talk about the campus-wide protests and demonstrations that were spearheaded by students. It has been years since a "student takeover," and most campus issues are addressed through the Student Government Association. Most recently, Spelman students spoke out against the negative images of women in music videos. An invitation was extended to rap artist Nelly to come and discuss this issue, and he and his management team declined to attend. This led to some controversy in the media about Spelman not supporting Nelly's non-profit initiative to raise awareness around bone marrow donations; however, the Spelman community held its ground, specifying that they merely wanted Nelly to participate in a dialogue to address their concerns dealing with the portrayal of women in music-related media.

Gay Pride

The lesbian community on Spelman's campus is supported, and the organization Afrakete provides support and a "safe space" for gay, bisexual, and transgender students. Many students at Spelman do not talk openly about sexual orientation, and some believe that the school, as well as Morehouse, are subject to generalizations and rumors that exaggerate the number of gay students, merely because they are same-sex schools.

Economic Status

Spelman has students from all socioeconomic backgrounds; however, there is the stereotype that all students who attend Spelman come from wealthy families. Eight-five percent of Spelman students receive some form of financial aid.

Minority Clubs

As a Historically Black College/University (HBCU) Spelman's minority clubs are structured differently than at other institutions. There is a large percentage of students who come from other states, and for many years there have been state clubs so that students can meet others from the same general area. Some of the more prominent clubs are the California Club, the Tri-State Club, and the Texas Club. There is also a club for international students. There are also a number of religious groups on campus. These include Al Nissa, an organization for Muslim women, the AUC Baha'I Club, and Campus Crusade for Christ.

Most Common Religions

Christianity is popular, as well as Islam.

Students Speak Out On...
Diversity

"I find it very diverse, especially with exchange programs. I met five or six exchange students on an international level. I got to see what other cultures thought of African Americans."

Q "Even though Spelman is predominantly an African American all-girls school, there is diversity. **There are various religions, cultures, geographic locations**, shades, sizes, and outlooks that can be found at Spelman. In addition, some Spelman students and exchange students from Occidental are of different races and nationalities to add to Spelman's uniqueness. I never once felt that everyone is the same on campus. There are always new people to meet with new perspectives to add to any conversation. The professors and administrators are a good representation of diversity, being African American, African, West Indian, Indian, Middle Eastern, Asian, and white."

Q "Some people who haven't attended an HBCU might say that there isn't much diversity, but to say that about Spelman would be totally inaccurate. You meet so many women from different parts of the country, from different religions, and from different walks of life. Just by walking around, you'll notice that people have so many different styles. **I think it's one of the most diverse settings for black women**."

Q "You have students who grew up in all-white neighborhoods or all black. **You have students from different socioeconomic backgrounds**. Although it is predominantly African American, I feel it is diverse."

Q "The campus is very diverse. **The rumor that all Spelman women are alike is simply that—a rumor**. I have met so many different women from all over the U.S. and from other countries. I appreciated the diversity, because I learned so much from my peers that I may not have learned anywhere else."

Q "Some are cool and laid-back, and **some are narrow-minded and Afrocentric**."

Q "**You have students from all over the world**. There is also a great deal of diversity on the faculty."

Q "Very diverse, even though it is all black women. **We have students who come from other places or transfer**."

Q "Well of course, racially, there is no real diversity, but **we do have diversity when it comes to socioeconomic backgrounds**. All Spelmanites were 'that girl' in high school who knew she was going places. We are all on that same level in that respect. As far as where we lived and where we have been, that is where diversity comes in."

Q "Spelman is an all-female and historically black institution, but there is still every single person you can think of. Diversity isn't always about ethnicity. **People come from all types of areas and backgrounds**. Everyone has their own story. In that way, Spelman has a lot of diversity. At Spelman, you are able to have your own mind and form your own opinions."

Q "I think it is very diverse. **People think that it's an all black school**. I tell them everybody is so different."

The College Prowler Take On...
Diversity

There are many elements to diversity, including ethnicity, age, economic status, sexuality, family structure, and major. At Spelman, there seems to be general agreement that, from a racial standpoint, there is not a great deal of visible diversity. However, many students tend to agree that defining diversity one dimensionally by race will not give you a clear picture of the distinct differences among the population. The women at Spelman believe there is diversity predominantly because all of the students have a different background, be that with respect to family, money, interests, politics, or experiences. There are no carbon copies amongst these women, and they are actually taught from day one to be individuals and stand up for themselves, as well as their beliefs.

Spelman participates in exchange programs that bring students from other schools and other countries to the campus. In the Continuing Education Program, there are also students who attend Spelman who might be returning to school later in life, bringing with them the diversity of their age. From a state makeup, Spelman also has a good mix of people from the North, South, East, and West. The cultural norms in these regions of the United States are different and create a unique Spelman culture that is a fusion of distinct tastes in apparel, political views, music, hair styles, and so on.

The College Prowler® Grade on
Diversity: D+

A high grade in Diversity indicates that ethnic minorities and international students have a notable presence on campus and that students of different economic backgrounds, religious beliefs, and sexual preferences are well-represented.

Guys & Girls

The Lowdown On...
Guys & Girls

Male Undergrads:
Less than 1%

Female Undergrads:
99%

Birth Control Available?
Yes

Social Scene
Students are very social and involved on Spelman's campus. There is always something going on, and students, both men and women, from surrounding campuses will come over to check out the activities. The Student Government Association promotes the open-air vendor exposé known as Market Friday

(Social Scene, continued)

at the Student Center, and everyone is out and about on that day, especially the Greeks. Freshman year, students tend to make the friends that will stick with them throughout their time at Spelman. You can meet some upperclasswomen in some of your courses who will let you into their group of friends. The same thing is true with students who have the same majors, as you will find those who study together, socialize together. Joining clubs and staying active will help you to branch out.

Hookups or Relationships?

The Atlanta University Center is home to all sorts of relationships. Both hookups and relationships are prevalent, and it seems to really just depend on the individuals. There are some people who will meet their future spouse the first week at Spelman and others who will play the field and have a good time.

Dress Code

There is no dress code at Spelman. For the most part, it is a fashion show filled with different tastes. You'll have the ladies who wear sweatpants everyday and the ones who prefer to dress business casual. You'll find tank tops, skirts, and sandals in the summer. You'll have those who wear Afrocentric garb and others who design their own clothes. It is like a multicultural mall full of different styles on Spelman's campus.

Did You Know?

Top Places to Find Hotties:
1. Market Friday
2. "The Strip" at neighboring Clark Atlanta University
3. Greek events

Top Places to Hook Up:
1. Off-campus parties
2. Off-campus residences
3. At Morehouse or Clark Atlanta University
4. Basically, anywhere but on Spelman's campus!

Students Speak Out On...
Guys & Girls

> "There aren't any guys. In general, the Morehouse guys are short. You will think they are hot after you graduate."

Q "Being in the AUC was a unique experience because **I got to meet a ton of different guys** from different backgrounds with differing goals. The dating scene can be intense because of the close proximity of the schools and occurrences of conflicts over relationships. But the guys are great as friends and for networking. In general, the student bodies in the local schools are intelligent, fun, and easy to get along with. Students got together for fun and for studying."

Q "**The guys at Morehouse are very friendly**. There are many cute guys around, but be careful, because they can be dogs."

Q "The guys are pretty attractive at other schools. At Spelman, **a lot of our male interaction is with Morehouse men**, and while there are a lot of cute guys, due to the small size of our schools, you tend to see the same eligible guys all the time. So the more you get off campus, the more variety you get."

Q "The guys at nearby schools are just like any other guy. **You have your nice guys and not-so-nice guys**. With them going to the institutions that they go to, maybe they feel like they should be seen in a certain way. They just really are average, run-of-the-mill guys, and that is how you have to treat them. I don't interact with students from other institutions. I don't engage with GA Tech or GA State that often."

Q "**Guys nearby are cool** and have heavy participation in our events."

Q "**The guys are just like guys** anywhere else."

Q "The guys at Morehouse are a little more gentlemanly, but at the same time, the school makes them more cocky than confident. They are more gentlemanly than the guys at CAU, who are more down-to-earth. The Clark Atlanta guys are more approachable than the ones at Morehouse, but they are not as chivalrous. I feel like it is the same way with the girls at other schools. We run into people from Emory. The girls seem pretty much the same as girls at Spelman, who think highly of themselves. In general, the people at Clark are more approachable. They seem more eager to talk to people than the people at Spelman. **Local Atlanta guys are aggressive**. "

Q "Well, **you have classes with a lot of guys from Morehouse**, which didn't make Spelman feel like an all-girls school."

Q "The relationship between Spelman and Morehouse is good. Guys are guys. **They are very social with females**. Spelman is a pretty friendly atmosphere."

Q "The guys are very happy because they have so much to choose from. **They are just like regular college guys, not looking to settle down**. You have disrespectful ones and respectful ones. At the surrounding schools the people are cool. There is still some tension between Spelman and Clark because of old things. I can tell individuals are trying to break down the barriers, but sometimes people have preconceived notions. I see people trying to work together on things. For parties, we will have people promote the unity."

Q "**I definitely don't agree with the stereotype that Spelman girls are stuck up**. I think it is more pronounced because it is a same-sex school. This goes along with the homosexual stereotype. I think we have the same percentage as other schools."

Q "I would say, depending on the institution, there is an air. Morehouse men have an air about them. **They are a little more uptight**. Some might say that about the women at Spelman."

The College Prowler Take On...
Guys & Girls

The dating scene on Spelman and in the surrounding Atlanta University Center is always full of surprises. There are definitely a number of people looking to date or find serious relationships, and there is another group of both men and women looking to hook up for the short term. The schools in the AUC have a history that goes back pretty far, and there are some "old school" stereotypes that have survived the test of time through word of mouth. Most people who spread the stereotypes about Morehouse men, Spelman women, or CAU students probably don't have friends outside of their own institution. Be careful not to fall prey to rumors and gossip.

The consensus seems to be that guys and girls are nice, but anyone can be up to no good. Taking time to get to know someone is advised. Spelman, as well as the other schools in the AUC, advocate safe sex and provide students with information and contraception. It is probably safe to say that there isn't a great deal of sexual activity between men and women on Spelman's campus, due to the fact that men are not allowed to spend the night. Also, once you live off campus, you can pretty much see whoever you want whenever you want. Overall, though, there seems to be no short supply of attractive, eligible, and ambitious bachelors.

The College Prowler® Grade on Guys: C

A high grade for Guys indicates that the male population on campus is attractive, smart, friendly, and engaging, and that the school has a decent ratio of guys to girls.

The College Prowler® Grade on Girls: B+

A high grade for Girls not only implies that the women on campus are attractive, smart, friendly, and engaging, but also that there is a fair ratio of girls to guys.

Athletics

The Lowdown On...
Athletics

Athletic Division:
NCAA Division III

Conference:
Great South

Colors:
Columbia blue

School Mascot:
Jaguar

Women's Varsity Sports:
Basketball
Cross-Country
Golf
Soccer
Tennis
Track & Field
Volleyball

Club Sports:
Cheerleading

Intramurals:
Currently, there are no formal intramural sports, although students and administration are working to bring them to the campus.

Athletic Fields
Read Hall Gymnasium

Getting Tickets
There generally are not a large number of spectators at the game. Finding tickets or a seat will not be difficult. Admission is generally free or a nominal charge.

Most Popular Sports
Although sports overall do not receive a great deal of support from the student body, the most popular are basketball, tennis, and volleyball.

Best Place to Take a Walk
The Oval, located in the middle of campus

Most Overlooked Teams

Most students would say all of them; however, golf and soccer might top the list. Some students are unaware that there is a soccer team.

Gyms/Facilities

Read Hall Gymnasium

Read Hall is home to the Maguerite F. Simon Gymnasium, and it houses the dance, athletics, and health and physical education programs. The gym is regulation size and has seating for spectators. The facility also contains a swimming pool, four tennis courts, a fitness center, a weight room, a bowling alley, a billiard center, three dance studios, an athletic training room, and women's and men's locker rooms. The gym is on the small side, and students generally feel it needs to be updated with new equipment. Other students believe that the hours that the gym is open make it inaccessible to students who are looking to work out after 9 p.m. in the evenings. The workout facility is also closed Friday through Sunday. See the Facilities section for student feedback regarding the gym.

Students Speak Out On...
Athletics

> "Athletics are not at all big on campus. I think people play basketball sometimes, but it's not organized. The only game that attracts a lot of people is the Spelman versus Bennett basketball game."

Q "The Spelman Jaguars are great! **The teams are a great way to have fun** and work your body, and the coaches are supportive and encouraging. We have basketball, volleyball, tennis, golf, and soccer teams. It depends on the sport as to whether or not there is a varsity team versus an IM team."

Q "**Varsity sports are not such a big deal**. We attend all of Morehouse's football and basketball games for entertainment and to see people."

Q "**Varsity sports aren't that big on campus**. There are basketball, volleyball, golf, track and soccer teams, but they aren't very big around campus. While Spelman doesn't have IM sports, Morehouse does, and students from Spelman often attend those games in addition to their varsity games."

Q "Varsity sports aren't very popular on campus. **We don't offer that many IM sports**. People start their own. At one time there was powder-puff football. Most individuals don't know we have a soccer or volleyball team. Publicity for them isn't big, and sports are not financially supported. The basketball team has better supplies than the golf or volleyball teams. We don't have our own stadium and have to use Morris Brown's for soccer."

Q "**No, there aren't any IM sports**. SGA is working on it."

Q "They are not big at all with me. With the campus they are not. **No one plans to go to a game unless it is a big rival school**. I would never go to a basketball game, only because I am not interested. With Morehouse it is different. Maybe I am not a school spirit person."

Q "IM sports are nonexistent. **Varsity sports don't get much support at all**. The good athletes don't come, nor those who really have a love for sports. That area needs improvement. The facilities aren't what they should be."

Q "Varsity sports are not popular at all. You do have student athletes. No one goes to support the athletes, which is important. Games are not very well publicized, and women's athletics are not as supported as they should be, in general. **When you play sports at Spelman, you don't get any scholarship money**. I don't know of any intramural sports."

Q "IM sports do not exist. I know our current SGA president is trying to get them, but the school is not being responsive. The athletic program is getting stronger. We are now Division III, and we have made changes to the department to meet the requirements. **The volleyball and basketball teams are the biggest sports**. As an ex-member of the tennis team, that is a rigorous program. They see us as scholar athletes, so they put academics first at all times. They don't discourage people from participating in sports, though it is a selective process."

Q "There isn't a great emphasis on sports, which is kind of sad because some people come looking for sports activities. **Spelman is working hard to put more spotlight on the sports scene**. In the past, this just hasn't been a big thing at Spelman."

The College Prowler Take On...
Athletics

Athletics is second to academics at Spelman, which some might argue is a good thing. However, there are many students who believe more emphasis and support should be given to sports programs. While there are teams and sporting events for the Jaguars, many students don't have an interest in attending or don't even know the schedule because of poor publicity. It appears that some students in leadership have put this on their radar screen and are not only seeking to help out in the varsity sport arena but are working toward launching IM sports on campus.

It seems as if there are some ad hoc IM and club sports that go on through smaller groups. A couple that students will mention are a powder-puff football team and a walking club. Students at Spelman are required to take at least two physical education courses as well, which may lead to practice outside of the regular class time. Along with the sports marketing and fan attendance issues, the athletic facilities are not state-of-the-art. Many regular students and athletes are not happy with the gymnasium or the equipment to be found there. For the most part, even with the recent promotion to Division III, the school has a long way to go in the athletic department.

The College Prowler® Grade on Athletics: C-

A high grade in Athletics indicates that students have school spirit, that sports programs are respected, that games are well-attended, and that intramurals are a prominent part of student life.

Nightlife

The Lowdown On...
Nightlife

Club and Bar Prowler:
Popular Nightlife Spots!

Club Crawler:

The club scene in Atlanta is varied. There are some clubs that are like lounges, and others where the dance floor is jumpin'! Recently, Atlanta has seen a number of South Beach-inspired places spring up, with outdoor patios, white furniture and cabanas for private

(Club Crawler, continued)

groups. As far as specials, these are few and far between. If you want a cheap drink, stay away from the clubs and go to a restaurant or bar. Also, try to look out for parties hosted by AUC students, alumni, or promoters. Chances are, you will get a good discount off regular night admission.

Apache Café
64 3rd St., Midtown
(404) 876-5436
www.apachecafe.info

(Apache Café, continued)

Apache Café is that chill spot where you can catch an underground artist or a spoken word set. The admission is usually nominal, and most nights there is a good crowd.

Specials: Art Mondays have a $3 donation at the door admission cost.

Babylon

3073 Peachtree Rd., Buckhead
(404) 869-1511

Babylon is another recent club conversion. Last year, this spot had a different name and a different decorator. Now this club is on the cutting edge with over 40 flat-screen televisions lining the wall and plenty of flashing lights to get your head spinning before you take a sip of your first drink. Many college promoters host parties here, so look out for the flyers.

Specials: Thursday night there is free admission and drink specials for the ladies.

Compound

1008 Brady Ave.
(404) 872-4621

Compound is one of the newest clubs in the Atlanta scene. Located in an old warehouse district, you will feel like you are at a trendy resort, as the front half of the club is situated outdoors. There are plenty of spaces to explore in this spread-out sanctuary for

(Compound, continued)

the trendy and the tasteful. No specials here, unless someone from the AUC is hosting the party. Be prepared to pay at the door for most events, but despite the cost, this is a club you want to get into, even as a broke college student.

Club 112

1055 Peachtree St., Midtown
(404) 607-7277

Immortalized in songs by some of today's best Atlanta hip-hop artists, 112, also known as "One Tweezy," has moved from Buckhead to Midtown, right across from its competitor, Vision Nightclub. The major draw of this club is the relaxed dress code and the fact that it stays open as late as 7 a.m. on some nights! Definitely the spot for the after-party!

Specials: On Wednesdays women can get in at a discount or free.

Frequency

220 Pharr Rd., Buckhead
(404) 760-1975

Frequency is another spot where you will find AUC parties. Greeks will host parties here from time to time as well. Look out for flyers and announcements. Parking in Buckhead is less than desirable, but if you get in free, it is worth it.

Havana Club

247 Buckhead Ave., Buckhead

(404) 869-8484

Havana Club boasts salsa dancing lessons for all levels and a unique cigar bar.

Leopard Lounge

84 12th St., Midtown

(404) 874-2704

www.leopardlounge.biz

Leopard Lounge is a great weekday hangout. Generally, they don't charge a cover, and you can get a good drink at a decent price. Going to Leopard Lounge is like going to that friend's place in high school whose parents were never home. They've got plenty of rooms you can explore unsupervised, and they won't get mad if you sit on the couch with a drink in your hand. Have fun and enjoy some amusing party people-watching (as people come and go from Vision Nightclub) from the porch.

Vision

1068 Peachtree St., Midtown

(404) 874-4460

www.visionatlanta.com

Vision is in the heart of the midtown club district and is one of the largest and most popular clubs in the city. It recently closed down for about three months to have a rumored million-plus-dollar makeover. The new look of

(Vision Nightclub, continued)

the club lands somewhere between South Beach and Las Vegas. Either way, you'll feel like you've been transported to another place once you step through the doors. If you are VIP, you may be partying with Diddy, Beyonce, or Usher, who have all been seen in the club. If you are on the e-mail list, you will find yourself receiving announcements or VIP e-mail passes that grant free admission for some nights, particularly Fridays. You must be dressed appropriately to get in.

Specials: Free admission with e-mail on Friday nights with LIVE Broadcast on V103FM hosted by Frank Ski and Ryan Cameron.

Whiskey Peach

44 12th St., Midtown

(404) 745-9551

www.whiskeypeach.com

They tag themselves as a "sleek, modern ultra-lounge" on their Web site. This is another venue of choice for Atlanta's promoters. Visit the Web site and look out for e-mails or flyers about the next party at this spot.

Bar Prowler:

The line between restaurants, bars, and clubs in Atlanta is blurred. Oftentimes, you will find a line just to get into some of Atlanta's hippest restaurants that just so happen to have a trendy bar scene. Some restaurant and bar locations even charge admission on the weekend, even if you plan to buy dinner. This list will let you know the places to check out and how early to get there to avoid paying to get into a restaurant just to turn around and pay for food or drinks.

Bucket Shop
3475 Lenox Rd., Buckhead
(404) 261-9244
www.bucketshopcafe.com

You can not beat the Bucket Shop when it comes to a cheap drink, and they are open late!

Specials: Drink specials everyday, with mugs of Budweiser, Bud Light, Coors Light or Miller Lite for only $3.95.

Cherry Restaurant
1051 West Peachtree Rd., Midtown
(404) 872-2020
www.aboutcherry.com

Cherry is a restaurant and bar that doubles as a nightspot for various parties throughout the year.

Specials: Martinis are $3 on Monday.

Copeland's of New Orleans
3365 Piedmont Rd., Buckhead
(404) 475-1000
www.alcopeland.com

Copeland's generally has well-priced drinks, and on the weekends it turns into a club that student party promoters can afford to rent out.

Specials: The parties always have drink specials under $5.

Django
495 Peachtree St., Midtown
(404) 347-8648
www.djangoatlanta.com

They serve food here, but most people know it as a bar and party spot. Promoters will rent out the event space downstairs, known as "the Belly" and throw parties. There is a bar downstairs and a DJ booth, and for a restaurant/bar, a nice amount of space and seating. You can meet and drink late! Django is open until 3 a.m.

Luxe Restaurant
89 Park Place, Downtown
(404) 389-0800

Specials: Another hotspot for college and Homecoming parties, as Luxe has a private room upstairs. The bar is a great place to have an intimate drink with someone special.

Shout

1197 Peachtree St., Midtown

(404) 846-2000

www.heretoserve restaurants.com

The Here to Serve restaurant group has hit a goldmine. Two of their restaurants have emerged as the top hangout spots in Atlanta and are places to see and be seen. Shout is in the heart of midtown and boasts a beautiful view of the city, great drinks, and two levels to party on. They bring in DJs during the weekend. The drawback is that on Fridays and Saturdays they have been known to charge admission. Arrive early to get in free and avoid drama at the door. Parking is also limited in the area, so be prepared to pay or walk several blocks.

Specials: Free admission everyday, but get there early on the weekends to avoid paying a cover.

Slice

259 Peters St., West End

(404) 588-1820

www.sliceatlanta.com

A DJ spins on many nights of the week. Admission is free, it is less than five minutes from the school, and you can get a pretty good slice of pizza!

Twist

3500 Peachtree Rd., Phipps Plaza, Buckhead

(404) 869-1191

www.heretoserver estaurants.com

Twist came first, then Shout, in the Here to Serve Restaurant Group. Now, not as popular as its counterpart, Twist is still a great place to get a martini. The sushi is great, too. They bring in a DJ on the weekends to keep the energy high and the chance of you leaving for the club low.

Specials: Free admission every night. Best advice is to get there early.

Student Favorites:
Babylon
Dragonfly
Frequency
Whiskey Peach

Other Places to Check Out:
Chocolate

Primary Areas with Nightlife:
Buckhead
Midtown

Cheapest Place to Get a Drink:
Bucket Shop

Bars Close At:
Some between 3 a.m.–4 a.m. in downtown Atlanta and 2 a.m.–3 a.m. in Buckhead

Local Specialties:
Green Apple Martini – a Southern favorite

Favorite Drinking Games:
Have You Ever?
Truth or Dare

Useful Resources for Nightlife

AJ Productions, Inc. includes both 18+ and 21+ parties attended by many AUC students (*www.ajpinc.net*).

Night Life Link is based out of Atlanta and keeps an extensive list of things going on in Atlanta (*www.nightlifelink.com*).

Prophecy Events is an Atlanta promoter with parties catered to upperclassman AUC students (*www.prophecy-events.com*).

Ticketmaster is great for concerts (*www.ticketmaster.com*).

Organization Parties

The Greeks throw parties, and they are usually very well attended. The Deltas have been known in the past to throw a tight Homecoming party and have booked such venues as Lakewood Amphitheatre, the Fox Theatre, and most of the hot Atlanta clubs. Some of the state organizations also throw parties that you don't want to miss. There is the infamous LATEX party, which is a collaboration between students from both Louisiana and Texas.

What to Do if You're Not 21

There are some clubs that will let you in even if you aren't 21. Try Buckhead. Also, most of the restaurant-bars will let you into the establishment, but you just won't be able to enjoy the libations! Places like the Tabernacle, Velvet Underground at Hard Rock Café, the Fox Theatre, Chastain Park, and Lakewood Amphitheatre have live shows you can attend. Here are a couple of coffeeshops that stay open a little later and are a tad bit trendier than the local Starbucks:

Café Intermezzo

1845 Peachtree Rd., Midtown

(404) 355-0411

You won't have to beg your way into this bistro if you are under 21. Of course, don't try to order any liquor, but with pages of non-alcoholic drinks and desserts you might get arrested for having a sugar high once you leave this place. It is cozy and intimate—perfect for a date or to impress someone who isn't familiar with the city. They stay open late, and there is always a wait after major concerts or when parties let out.

JavaVino

579 North Highland Ave.

(404) 577-8673

www.javavino.com

This is a cool, cozy place that doesn't card. Great for a quick cup of joe and a dessert. Also nice to go to with your 21-and-up friends who want a glass of wine but know you can't get into the regular bar and club scene.

Tarrazu

117 Martin Luther King Jr. Dr., Downtown

265 Ponce de Leon Ave., Midtown

(404) 815-2077

Tarrazu has two locations. They are a popular after-dinner spot to grab a glass of wine and a tasty dessert. They don't card, and you can be sure to have an entertaining evening, as they host some of the best jazz musicians in the city at both locations. Arrive early to get a seat, as space is limited. Admission is always free.

Specials: Spoken Word Sunday, Moet and a Movie Monday, Conversations Tuesday, Wine Down Wednesdays (wine tasting), and live jazz Thursday–Saturday

Students Speak Out On...
Nightlife

"**After the first two or three months of freshman year, I think all the partying is done off campus. The names of the spots keep changing, though, so I don't know where people who are under 21 go.**"

Q "There are only a few parties on campus, held in Lower Manley. **Most of the parties that we attended were at houses and apartments of other students** or at other schools in the AUC. But there is always something going on in ATL, so we didn't really miss not having a lot of parties on our own campus. The clubs are hot in ATL. You can find a lounge/chill spot, techno clubs, and clubs that play R&B, hip-hop, rap, go-go, reggae, Latin, and pop. There are clubs like 112 that are nationally known because of music artists performing and visiting. You can find upscale/dressier clubs and bars where you can wear jeans. All you have to do is decide what you want for the night (e.g., music, dress, and atmosphere), then go."

Q "Off campus, the places to go were Havana Club, Vision, and pretty much any club in Buckhead, especially around Pharr Road and Apache Café. Clubs in Atlanta tend to change names and genre pretty frequently, so you have to watch out for that. One year it could be a R&B/hip-hop club, and you come back from summer break and it's a gay country bar or something. **You figure out what places to go by the radio and party fliers**."

Q "The parties on campus were fun; however, **the sororities and fraternities had the best parties at local hotels**, usually downtown. Transportation is usually provided."

Q "Students are always well-informed about the parties on and off campus via flyers and posters. **You can always find something to do on the weekends**."

Q "Parties on campus are great. **They are almost always freshman-oriented**, but it gives you an opportunity to become familiar with your classmates while having lots of fun. They are great in the wintertime, also, because you don't have to worry about waiting outside in the cold to get into the clubs."

Q "**Freshman parties in Lower Manley were so much fun**! Then we graduated to the club scene in and around ATL."

Q "**Parties on campus are loosely chaperoned**. You are restricted to people in the AUC. Off campus is a whole new ball game. There are people from CAU, GA Tech, and Emory. There is more diversity. Hotspots are Vision and Club 112, but they are 21 and up. The college clubs don't last long and are always changing. There is a newer one called Chocolate."

Q "There is always a party to go to, and they will have a shuttle to take you to clubs in the city. **Usually, it is still an all-AUC crowd and mostly college students**. Good spots are Babylon, Cherry, and Copeland's. Most of the parties you will find out because you know the people throwing them."

Q "Parties on campus are whack. They end early. The security guards are out of control with the guys. No one goes to those, unless it is at Morehouse or CAU. Off-campus parties are excellent. **Everybody goes, depending on who hosts them**."

Q "I don't go to AUC parties that much anymore because **you see the same people over and over**."

Q "Market Friday is sort of a party. Off campus, the parties are fine. If you go with a group of friends, you will have a good time. Locations are prime; even if you don't want to go to the party, you will find something to do in the area where the party is. **Cover charges aren't outrageous.**"

Q "Off campus, people like to go to **Babylon, as well as Luxe, which is actually a restaurant.**"

Q "**Off-campus parties are always an experience with the shuttle situations**. Get there early to get on, and don't miss the last one back to campus. Don't wait for the last one, because you might not get on it, and you'll have to take a cab home."

The College Prowler Take On...
Nightlife

Nightlife on campus leaves a little to be desired after you have graduated from the Lower Manley Student Center parties that were so fun freshman year. The next big thing for the sophomores is to take the chartered bus to the local club for AUC parties. Promoters arrange for buses to pick students up at various locations, including right outside of Spelman's gates. There have been times when you would think the bus was taking people to see Oprah or Diddy the way people flock to get on. These parties are generally for 18-and-ups and are low cost.

For those who are 21 and up, Atlanta has much to offer. There are clubs, lounges, trendy restaurants, and bars that take on a club-like atmosphere on the weekends. There are three ways that people in the AUC generally find out about the hype parties: e-mail lists/Web sites, hand flyers, and radio. Another way people find out is because they know the promoter throwing the party. The sororities are known for throwing the parties that everyone wants to be at. The chapters at Spelman have a long-standing history of attracting huge crowds just by having their name on the flyer. Some of the best spots for the college crowd include Babylon and Frequency. The only problem with the Atlanta nightlife scene is that clubs change names and themes so much that it is often hard to keep up. In general, however, nightlife is great, and you will find that you are never at a loss for options.

The College Prowler® Grade on
Nightlife: A-

A high grade in Nightlife indicates that there are many bars and clubs in the area that are easily accessible and affordable. Other determining factors include the number of options for the under-21 crowd and the prevalence of house parties.

Greek Life

The Lowdown On...
Greek Life

Number of Sororities:
4

Undergrad Women in Sororities:
5%

Sororities:
Alpha Kappa Alpha
Delta Sigma Theta
Sigma Alpha Iota Music Fraternity
Zeta Phi Beta

Honors Socieities:
Alpha Epsilon Delta
Alpha Lambda Delta
Alpha Sigma Lambda
Beta Kappa Chi
Kappa Delta Epsilon
Phi Beta Kappa
Pi Sigma Alpha
Psi Chi
Sigma Tau
Upsilon Pi Epsilon

Did You Know?

You can't join a sorority at Spelman until your sophomore year or until you have received sophomore status.

Students Speak Out On...
Greek Life

> "Greek life is very prevalent on Spelman's campus. I wouldn't go as far as to say that it dominates the social scene, however there is an impact."

Q "**The sororities at Spelman are serious**. Alpha Kappa Alpha Sorority Inc. and Delta Sigma Theta Sorority Inc. are the most prevalent. They hold lots of events and parties and help organize great volunteering opportunities. But since a large number of ladies never pledge, it is a great balance. If you do or don't, there is still a crowd for you."

Q "**Greek life is very active on campus**. However, so is the freshman dorm scene, which prevents domination from occurring."

Q "I didn't really participate in the Greek life, so **it didn't dominate my world**."

Q "It is basically like a big circle of friends. If you are Greek, it's like people will automatically be your friend. **It has become sort of elitist**."

Q "Greek life doesn't dominate the social scene, but **it does play a big part**."

Q "**Greek life had a positive impact on campus life**. I pledged in a sorority; however, I had many friends who did not, yet they still thoroughly enjoyed their Spelman experience."

Q "**It is very exclusive**. Sometimes, it seems as if the Greeks as a whole are somewhat united. I think they socialize with other Greeks more than those who aren't Greek, but maybe it just seems that way. By having Greek life, it adds more depth to the social life here."

Q "Deltas throw the best parties. **Deltas dominate the campus in every way**. But by no means do you have to be Greek to have a great experience."

Q "I wouldn't say it dominates the social scene. We are seen as the leaders on campus, but at the same time, **we respect the bigger sisterhood that is the Spelman sisterhood**. The different organizations get along. We don't have problems between us. We respect each other."

Q "There are many who participate in Greek life, but **you can still have a life without it**."

Q "**Greek life dominates the social scene 100 percent**. I don't like it, but I think if there is something Greek going on, everyone flocks to it. It's not good, but it's what happens. I think it happens at all black schools."

Q "I don't think that Greek life dominates the social scene, but **it is there, and it adds to campus life**."

Q "Greek life is dominant on Spelman's campus, but **you do not have to be Greek to have fun**. I had friends who were Greek and friends who weren't, and we both had equal fun during our college experience."

Q "I don't think it dominates the scene. There are a lot of times you know they are present. At senior party, people were making their organization calls. **You know they are there, but people aren't upset about their presence**."

The College Prowler Take On...
Greek Life

Greek life is a clear and dynamic presence on Spelman's campus, and they are responsible for a number of activities that promote sisterhood and community service. From forums on relationships to politics, they keep the campus engaged in all that is relevant to African American women. Spelman keeps a close watch on Greek activities and only allows women who have reached sophomore status to pledge. They also cap the number of students who can pledge in any given year. There are no Greek houses on campus, but many Greeks congregate at Market Fridays in the student center. You can spot them in their jackets or wearing the colors of their organizations. Many times, sorority and visiting fraternity members from Morehouse or Clark Atlanta University will engage in impromptu displays on campus. There are annual AUC step shows, and Spelman's chapters have a history of competing and sometimes taking home top honors and bragging rights when it is all over.

The Greeks are known to throw the best parties and social events as well, especially during Homecoming. It is not unusual for alumnae to come back for Homecoming and ask "Where is the Delta party this year?" or "Did the AKAs win the step show?" All of the women at the school are united through their Spelman experiences and traditions.

The College Prowler® Grade on
Greek Life: A

A high grade in Greek Life indicates that sororities and fraternities are not only present, but also active on campus. Other determining factors include the variety of houses available and the respect the Greek community receives from the rest of the campus.

Drug Scene

The Lowdown On...
Drug Scene

Most Prevalent Drugs on Campus:
None, really. Liquor seems to be the one that people are brave enough to consistently attempt to bring on campus.

Liquor-Related Referrals:
6

Liquor-Related Arrests:
0

Drug-Related Referrals:
1

Drug-Related Arrests:
0

Drug Counseling Programs

Students may find information regarding counseling and treatment for drug and alcohol additions from College Health Services, College Counseling Services, or the Office of Student Affairs. Workshops are held to address substance abuse issues, and there are steps to intervene if you have concerns about a friend or roommate.

Students Speak Out On...
Drug Scene

"We have a pretty dry campus. People do drink when they go out. I don't see anyone drinking on campus. Even people smoking on campus seems weird. People just don't seem to do it."

Q "**Drugs are easy to obtain and easy to avoid**, it all depends on where you go and whom you decide to hang out with."

Q "**Spelman is pretty strict with any violation, so the use of drugs would be too much of a gamble**. You can't even smoke cigarettes out in the open at school. Now, off campus, there is probably more drug use because there is more privacy, but I honestly didn't see too much of that. If you're going to consider alcohol a drug, people will drink on campus quicker than they will smoke weed, for example. Drinking happens usually before people go out to the club ('pre-gaming'). The theory is you have enough drinks to get you tipsy at home (which is economical), then you only have to buy one or two drinks at the club to 'set you over.' But, of course, bottles aren't left out in the open, and people are discrete, because Spelman is a dry campus."

Q "I recall a student getting caught with marijuana. **It was a major deal**."

Q "There was a lot of weed smoking, but **I never felt forced to get high**. I didn't encounter many other kinds of drug use."

Q "Drugs are everywhere in the world, but **not too much was available at Spelman, outside of weed**, and that wasn't often."

Q "**They smoke a lot of weed**. People drink, but not too many other drugs."

Q "I personally can't say much about it. I haven't seen anyone doing crack. At parties, I have seen people smoking weed, or at after-parties. **I have experienced drug usage at other schools in the AUC**."

Q "When you get to college, **everyone drinks, and it is part of life**. As far as excessive drinking goes, I don't think it's that bad."

Q "Since I have been at Spelman I have only heard of one incident where there was a group of guys and girls smoking weed. **I am sure there are students that engage in drug activity, but not as much on campus**."

Q "I personally would say that it exists, but **it's not brought into the day to day**. People do it, but no one talks about it."

The College Prowler Take On...
Drug Scene

Drugs, specifically hard drugs, do not have a visible presence on campus. It seems as if drug use is limited, or people are very discrete about it. Almost everyone has a story about the "girl who got caught with weed." Maybe Public Safety just keeps telling the same story every year to keep people from thinking they can get away with bringing any contraband onto campus! Despite being a dry campus, it sounds like every now and again people may partake in a few alcoholic libations in the dorm room prior to going out to a party or a club. However, this still seems to be rather taboo on campus and is reserved more for off-campus gatherings.

The drug scene outside of some who smoke marijuana or drink liquor and beer is seemingly nonexistent. Even those who have witnessed drug use at parties only mentioned those two types of activity. Most of the drinking amongst Spelman students takes place during key events, such as Greek Week, Senior Week, Homecoming, and graduation weekend. Homecoming is the only weekend when there is a major tailgate party with liquor flowing more readily because of the presence of Morehouse and Spelman alumni on the campus and surrounding property. Spelman seems to be a relatively drug-free campus with only certain students who participate in the heavy drug and alcohol scene.

The College Prowler® Grade on

Drug Scene: A

A high grade in the Drug Scene indicates that drugs are not a noticeable part of campus life; drug use is not visible, and no pressure to use them seems to exist.

Campus Strictness

The Lowdown On...
Campus Strictness

What Are You Most Likely to Get Caught Doing on Campus?

- Letting a guy spend the night
- Drinking or doing drugs on campus out in the open
- Smoking cigarettes in your room
- Letting a commuter live in your room
- Parking your car illegally or leaving it on campus too long
- Burning candles or incense in your room
- Cooking in your room
- Damaging furniture in the dorm or in your room
- Moving furniture from the lounges into your room

Students Speak Out On...
Campus Strictness

"They are very strict. Our freshman year, some girls were smoking in the dorm, and they got in big trouble. In a matter of minutes the whole school knew. They don't play."

Q "It depends on what your offense is and what officer it is. **Drugs hold a heavier stigma than alcohol**, so I could imagine if an officer found weed on you, there would probably be consequences. If you're 21 and are intoxicated on campus, unless there is alcohol currently on you, there isn't much that can be said. But to be real truthful, the police tend to stay in their security booths, so it's pretty hard to get caught if you're in the privacy of your own room."

Q "**It is definitely a no tolerance policy**. If you are out in the open with it, you will be punished or even arrested."

Q "**I imagine that they are strict**, but I've never had to deal with it."

Q "I am told they are strict; however, **I don't recall any specific run-ins or problems when I was at Spelman**. I do remember coming back to campus after several parties having had too much to drink and stumbling across campus with my roommate and friends, but there were never any altercations or events that stand out in my mind with regard to drugs or drinking while I was there."

Q "They are very strict on drugs and drinking, as with any indecent behavior. **They won't tolerate misconduct**."

Q "**They are very strict** about drug use on campus."

Q "I haven't heard of too many incidents. I heard about one with people who had alcohol in the dorm, and **they were put on probation**."

Q "As far as campus police are concerned, **you can't walk on campus with an open bottle**. If they see someone with stuff, they will stop them."

Q "I don't think they are really strict. **They don't check your rooms like they say**. I think people can get away with it. I know over at Morehouse guys would have a lot of drinks in their rooms."

Q "They are strict, but if someone wants to do something, they will find a way. **It isn't hard to bring alcohol on campus**."

Q "Campus police are very strict. My freshman year, **two girls were caught with weed, and it was a big deal**. They were immediately reprimanded. The immediate response shows they are serious."

The College Prowler Take On...
Campus Strictness

Spelman's history of numerous rules and regulations automatically feeds the perception of being strict, and this perception is reflected at least in part by reality. The stories students tell about those who got caught do not end with a slight slap on the wrist. Instead, it sounds in most cases as if students were placed on probation, escorted off campus, or introduced to the Atlanta Police Department.

Some students believe that sneaking things like alcohol and weed on campus is easy, but even if it is, many agree it is not worth the consequences. Since Spelman is such a small school, when someone is caught breaking a rule, even a small one, it is a matter of hours before the whole campus knows and the story is blown out of proportion. Just the idea of being the subject of daily gossip is enough to keep most students from breaking the rules. RAs and RDs take their jobs very seriously, and if they smell incense or a candle, even an aromatherapy one, they will reprimand you. If furniture goes missing from the study hall, eventually someone will come looking for that lamp or sofa you thought went so well with your bedspread. Don't even think about trying to sneak a man on campus. It is virtually impossible, as visitation is tightly monitored, and most dorms only have one way in and out outside of an emergency. It is best to just try to walk the straight line.

The College Prowler® Grade on
Campus Strictness: D

A high Campus Strictness grade implies an overall lenient atmosphere; police and RAs are fairly tolerant, and the administration's rules are flexible.

Parking

The Lowdown On...
Parking

Approximate Parking Permit Cost:
$350 per semester,
$700 per year

Parking Services:
AAA Parking
350 Spelman Lane
Campus Box 305
(404) 270-5431

Student Parking Lot?
Yes

Freshmen Allowed to Park?
No

Common Parking Tickets:
Expired Meter
Fire Lane
Handicapped Zone
No Parking Zone

Parking Permits

In order to keep your vehicle in the Spelman parking deck you must obtain a permit. There are only 180 spaces in the parking deck available to upperclasswomen. Permits are provided on a first-come, first-served basis, and payment is necessary in advance. Commuter students can use the deck at three dollars per day with no in and out privileges.

Did You Know?

Best Places to Find a Parking Spot:

The parking lots outside Spelman's gates, but you have to pay here. The parking deck also usually has slots open, but it has been known to fill to capacity.

Good Luck Getting a Parking Spot Here:

Any of the streets within walking distance of the school. Best bet is if you have an early morning class, you may find an open slot. People from big cities are used to parallel parking, but non-city folk struggle with the tight spaces. You'll learn how to get that SUV into a curbside spot quickly after being late for a couple of classes. Once you get street parking and can parallel park with your eyes closed, your luck might change, as many of the street parking areas are prone to vandalism.

Students Speak Out On...
Parking

"Parking is awful. First of all, it costs too much. When you tell people from other schools what you pay, they are floored. There isn't adequate parking. That is something that needs to be improved."

Q "There is mostly pay parking at Spelman. **There is no parking within the gates**, but since the campus is somewhat small, that's okay. There is a deck for students and teachers, and a swipe card for parking can be purchased through the school. There are also pay parking lots in front of the school and in other schools' lots. There is some street parking, but that usually fills up quick with commuters who have early morning classes and have to stay on campus all day."

Q "**It is very difficult to park**. Not enough parking."

Q "If you're on campus, parking is on the pricier side compared to other schools, but you're guaranteed a spot. Parking outside of the parking deck on campus is risky because you run the risk of getting violation stickers then being towed. **If you live off campus, parking becomes an art form that you must master**! First off, you have a commuter parking decal, which makes it tougher for you to get on campus at times. Secondly, you need to come early and hope the deck or the lots outside of Spelman aren't full. If those are full, you then have to drive around the AUC and try and find street parking or park at Morehouse's parking deck."

Q "It's easy to park if you sign a contract. **Daily parking can be a pain**."

Q "**There isn't enough free parking** around campus."

Q "It is not easy to park. **I feel like it is way too hard to park on campus because of the money**. A parking pass is $350 a semester to park in the deck. That is more than Clark and Morehouse parking. If you don't buy a pass, you have to pay three dollars a day to park. I feel like it is ridiculous. They only let faculty and staff park on campus. If you park there, you can get your car towed, which is another expense. Some people park on Lee Street and other streets. The risk they take is having their cars broken into. Cars get broken into everyday on certain streets."

Q "**Parking at Spelman is horrible**. Get to wherever you gotta go early, and bring money for the parking fee."

Q "**It is very expensive to park** on campus ($700 for the whole year)."

Q "Why they charge so much to park in the AUC is **beyond my comprehension**."

Q "**Parking is more or less a challenge for Monday, Wednesday, and Friday classes** when more students have scheduled classes."

Q "Parking is horrible on campus. **They charge an arm and a leg**. They tow people's cars, especially if you are parked on campus. You pay so much to go there, and they are quick to tow your cars. It is hard for commuter students, and sometimes on Wednesdays the parking deck is full."

Q "It is easy to park for me because I have a handicap sticker I got from someone. The thing about parking on our campus is that if you have a commuter sticker they will tow you. **Spelman will tow your car in a minute, and I think it's wrong**. Parking is too expensive, which is why I don't buy the permit."

Q "It isn't easy to park. The lots are always full, and **you find yourself driving around and around**."

Q "Oh gosh, no! It is horrible! The parking lots are owned by outside companies. They are not there for the best interest of the students. **There is very limited parking**. People park on the streets or West End, and sometimes cars get broken into. If you park in the lot, it is three dollars a day. You used to have an option to park in the Morehouse deck, but that was taken away. Sometimes I am late for class because of parking."

Q "Spelman does have a parking deck and front parking lots. **If you don't want to pay everyday, you can get the parking permits** or find parking on the street somewhere."

Q "No, it is not easy to park. It is three dollars a day. **Morehouse is a little cheaper**. A lot of people get up early to park on the street."

The College Prowler Take On...
Parking

If you could get a dollar for every student who has something negative to say about the parking situation at Spelman, you'd be a rich person. It is like finding a needle in a haystack to even find someone who doesn't use the word awful, horrible, or expensive when they describe the parking options they have on a day-to-day basis. Those who live off campus don't see the benefit of the yearly pass, especially if they only have classes on certain days, but the three-dollar charges add up, and the parking deck and lots are often full. There is parking in the surrounding neighborhoods, but there is a crime risk with that, and you have to get up at the crack of dawn to get a prime location.

Parking at the other schools and the associated prices may be driving the anger of some of the students. Morehouse and Clark Atlanta University are charging less to park. Some students complain that until recently they had the option to park at Morehouse, but because so many Spelman students were going over there, they had to discontinue it. The parking deck and surrounding lots on the Spelman campus appear to be under the control of a separate company, so it is unclear whether the institution can do anything about it. The bottom line is Spelman students find parking to be one of the least positive experiences at the college.

The College Prowler® Grade on
Parking: D-

A high grade in the Parking section indicates that parking is both available and affordable, and that parking enforcement isn't overly severe.

Transportation

The Lowdown On...
Transportation

Ways to Get Around Town:

On Campus
AUC Shuttle
There is a shuttle that will take you to all of the Atlanta University Center institutions, the Woodruff Library, three MARTA hub stations (including the West End MARTA Station), and the student residential apartments.

Public Transportation
Metropolitan Atlanta Rapid Transit Authority (MARTA)
www.itsmarta.com
Customer information line: (404) 848-5000

Taxi Cabs
Buckhead Safety Cab
(404) 233-1152
Checker Cab Co.
(404) 351-1111
Yellow Cab Co.
(404) 521-0200

Car Rentals

Alamo
local: (404) 530-2800
national: (800) 327-9633
www.alamo.com

Avis
local: (404) 659-4814
national: (800) 831-2847
www.avis.com

Budget
local: (404) 530-3000
national: (800) 527-0700
www.budget.com

Dollar
local: (404) 559-9457
national: (800) 800-4000
www.dollar.com

Enterprise
local: (404) 659-6050
national: (800) 736-8222
www.enterprise.com

Hertz
local: (404) 530-2925
national: (800) 654-3131
www.hertz.com

National
local: (404) 530-2800
national: (800) 227-7368
www.nationalcar.com

Best Ways to Get Around Town

Your car
Your friend's car
MARTA

Ways to Get Out of Town:

Airport

Hartsfield-Jackson International Airport

(800) 897-1910

Hartsfield-Jackson International Airport is about 16 miles from Spelman. You can get there in under 25 minutes by car.

Airlines Serving Atlanta

American Airlines
(800) 433-7300
www.americanairlines.com

Continental
(800) 523-3273
www.continental.com

Delta
(800) 221-1212
www.delta-air.com

Northwest
(800) 225-2525
www.nwa.com

Southwest
(800) 435-9792
www.southwest.com

TWA
(800) 221-2000
www.twa.com

United
(800) 241-6522
www.united.com

US Airways
(800) 428-4322
www.usairways.com

How to Get to the Airport

MARTA gets there in about 30 to 40 minutes.

Airport Shuttles will come to the campus. The Atlanta Link has a booth in the airport and keeps Spelman, Clark Atlanta University, Morehouse, and Morris Brown on its list of service areas.

A cab ride to the airport costs about $35.

The Atlanta Link
245 University Ave.
Atlanta
(404) 524-3400
(866) 545-9633

Greyhound

The Atlanta Greyhound Bus Terminal is located a few miles from campus. It is a five-minute ride by car.

Atlanta Greyhound Bus Terminal
232 Forsyth St.
Atlanta, GA 30303
(404) 584-1728
www.greyhound.com

Amtrak

The Atlanta Amtrak Train Station is less than 10 miles from campus. You can get there in 15 minutes or less, depending on the traffic.

Atlanta Amtrak Train Station
1688 Peachtree St., NW
Atlanta, GA 30309
(800) 872-7245
www.amtrak.com

Travel Agents

Carlson Wagonlit Travel
(770) 396-2000

Departures Travel Inc.
(404) 231-0339

Safeway Travel
(404) 235-3580

Students Speak Out On…
Transportation

> "Most freshman stick to taking the MARTA. It's not as advanced as the subways in NY or Boston, but it gets you to the places most people go in Atlanta."

Q "**The MARTA is a convenient rail and bus system** that can get you almost anywhere in the city, and even out to some suburbs. It is great for doing clubbing downtown, so you don't have to pay to park. Compared to some other major cities' rail systems, it is easy to use, cheap, and clean."

Q "The AUC shuttle will take you to the MARTA train station, but you can walk there or take the bus. You can't get everywhere, but **you can get to what you would need**."

Q "MARTA is close but **not convenient for getting around Atlanta**. Bus service takes too long."

Q "**The MARTA was a life-saver freshman year** since we couldn't have cars. I could take it to go to the mall or to work. I just didn't like the fact that I had to walk so far to get to the train station."

Q "**I don't think it is safe to walk to MARTA at night**, and it is not reliable. Get a car if you can."

Q "MARTA is very convenient. It was an easy way to get many places in Atlanta. **I did not have a car my first year and used MARTA frequently**."

Q "**It is convenient for most places in Atlanta**. If you are going to Decatur or Marietta, be prepared to take the bus and keep a schedule with you!"

Q "Public transportation is accessible; however, after freshman year, **it is easier to find transportation with friends who have cars**."

Q "I don't think MARTA is very reliable. **It doesn't take you enough places**. I only remember going to Lenox."

Q "For the most part, it is convenient. There are bus stops at almost every block. **MARTA is pretty dependable and safe**. I haven't seen a lot of bad situations with them."

Q "Before I had a car, it was hard to catch the shuttle to the MARTA station. **It could be better**."

Q "I think it's convenient. **I think MARTA is a pretty good system**. I am from St. Louis, and it isn't that good there. My freshman year, I rode it a lot."

Q "**MARTA is great and goes all over the city**. The station is close to campus. It is reliable."

Q "I don't like the MARTA. I did use it freshman year to get to the mall and sometimes the Georgia dome. **I didn't use it very often**."

The College Prowler Take On...
Transportation

Public transportation in Atlanta is fairly easy to navigate, and it will be your best friend freshman year. From Spelman you can take a 15-minute walk up to the West End Metropolitan Atlanta Rapid Transit Authority (MARTA) station. MARTA is Atlanta's train system which runs on north-south and east-west rails. It's affordable, and you can get to just about anywhere around downtown Atlanta. A round trip will not cost more than five dollars. In addition, MARTA offers a UPass for college students that provides unlimited access to the train for a low monthly fee. There are numerous bus stops along major streets, and you can catch the bus from the train station itself, too. Don't expect anything like the transportation in larger cities such as New York or Boston, though.

For out-of-town students, the MARTA rolls right into the airport, literally. You get off your plane, go to baggage claim, and take a short ride on the train. Spelman offers a free shuttle service to and from the West End MARTA station as well. Taxis are not as hard to come by in the city as they used to be, but if you do happen to have upperclassman friends, make sure to keep their numbers with you in the case that you are stranded and looking at a $50 cab fare. Overall, public transportation is convenient and reliable, but after freshman year, many students just get cars.

The College Prowler® Grade on Transportation: C

A high grade for Transportation indicates that campus buses, public buses, cabs, and rental cars are readily-available and affordable. Other determining factors include proximity to an airport and the necessity of transportation.

Weather

The Lowdown On...
Weather

Average Temperature:
Fall: 63 °F
Winter: 45 °F
Spring: 62 °F
Summer: 79 °F

Average Precipitation:
Fall: 3.62 in.
Winter: 4.51 in.
Spring: 4.32 in.
Summer: 4.14 in.

Students Speak Out On...
Weather

> "It is really, really hot in August, and it cools down after Labor Day. In the winter it can get pretty cold, so wear layers most of the time."

Q "**Atlanta has four complete seasons**. The summer is hot (thus the nickname HotLanta) and can be brutal in the un-air-conditioned dorms. The normal summer wear is a tank top and shorts. Autumn in Atlanta is funny; it can be really warm or kind of chilly, so it's good to not put your summer clothes up too early and not have your jackets too far away. Winter is mild, and if it snows, it's usually only like an inch or two. It gets cold like other Southern states, but it does not have winter-like weather as long or as severely as more northern states. The spring is perfect—warm days and cool nights."

Q "Atlanta consists of two seasons: hot and cold! Bring summer attire and winter attire. There is barely an in-between. People never believe how cold it gets at Spelman. **A lot of people don't realize it gets cold**, and one day it will be like 20 degrees out with no notice, and people will have to go out and buy coats and sweaters."

Q "The weather in Atlanta is almost always nice. There is about a month of really cold weather. **I would suggest that you bring a lot of sweaters and dress in layers,** because some days start out cool, and by the end of the day it will be warm again."

Q "**Usually, it is pretty hot**. I am from St. Louis, so I can wear shorts in the winter time. I don't know how others would dress. The winters do get cold, and summers get hot."

Q "The summer is hot and humid until around October. Then it gets cooler, and some years it snows. When it snows, it's usually not very much, but it can snow. **It stays cold until around April, when it warms to the 60s**. It's nice temperate weather, until June or July, when it heats up again. It rains alot in the summer and fall."

Q "The weather in Atlanta is **very hot during the summer**. Make sure you have enough cool clothing."

Q "On moving day, bring a tank top and shorts because you will be hot. **You will experience four seasons with no extremes, except the summer**."

Q "You should bring a variety of everything. **The weather is unpredictable and inconsistent**. One day it can be burning up, and the next day it's freezing cold."

Q "The weather is pretty nice. **It is really hot in the summertime with no air conditioning**. Bring plenty of shorts and tank tops. When it gets cooler, you have your jacket and sweatshirts. You won't need the bubble coats."

Q "**We do get a lot of rain**. Bring raincoat, umbrella, and galoshes!"

Q "From the time school starts until November it is pretty warm. I would say sandals, light jacket, jeans. After that, it gets really cold—not compared to Chicago, but **cold enough for a hat and coat**. By end of March and April, you can return to skirts and light jacket. By the time it hits May it is pretty warm."

The College Prowler Take On...
Weather

Atlanta doesn't have the nickname HotLanta for nothing! When you arrive for the fall semester, chances are, it will be blazing hot with temperatures in the 80s and 90s. Towards the end of the fall you will want to change into warmer attire. Many students wear sweats to class, but there are some occasions where you will have to attend mandatory freshman functions that will require you to wear business or business-casual clothing. On the weekend is mostly up to you, but one thing to note is that on Friday the campus hosts an outdoor market in the Student Center. If you are a trendsetter or you like to express yourself through what you wear, make sure to bring your best looks and save them for Market Friday.

The winter can be underestimated, especially by those students who come from the North and think that they don't need to cart down any of their winter sweaters or coats. You may not need to wear thermal underwear, but you will likely need a jacket with a little weight to it and boots during the winter. Spring is a time for colorful sundresses and skirts. The winter can be overcast and dreary, so when the sun comes back out most Spelman women welcome it with their best fashions. One item you need to always have as an optional part of your wardrobe is an umbrella. Atlanta gets much more rain than anyone ever expects.

The College Prowler® Grade on
Weather: A-

A high Weather grade designates that temperatures are mild and rarely reach extremes, that the campus tends to be sunny rather than rainy, and that weather is fairly consistent rather than unpredictable.

SPELMAN COLLEGE
Report Card Summary

ACADEMICS	B+
LOCAL ATMOSPHERE	A-
SAFETY & SECURITY	A+
COMPUTERS	B
FACILITIES	B-
CAMPUS DINING	C
OFF-CAMPUS DINING	A
CAMPUS HOUSING	B-
OFF-CAMPUS HOUSING	A+
DIVERSITY	D+
GUYS	C
GIRLS	B+
ATHLETICS	C-
NIGHTLIFE	A-
GREEK LIFE	A
DRUG SCENE	A
CAMPUS STRICTNESS	D
PARKING	D-
TRANSPORTATION	C
WEATHER	A-

Overall Experience

Students Speak Out On...
Overall Experience

"I'm happy that I chose Spelman. From my experience there and around the AUC, I'm a better person. I met a lot of lifelong friends, and hopefully my daughter will be able to attend!"

Q "I do not wish I was somewhere else. I have enjoyed my Spelman experience, and I am a junior. **I always wanted to go here, and my expectations have been met**, which is a blessing. Of course, there are small things that may happen. Coursework is hard. Other than that, I made a great decision."

Q "I love Spelman. **I wouldn't trade it for a million dollars**. Who knows? I could have ended up somewhere else, but God knew what He was doing."

Q "Spelman is hands down the best place for any woman, but especially women of color. Spelman does an excellent job of molding strong women and fostering esteem. **Being a woman of color is celebrated, discussed, and analyzed in a way that isn't done in our society**. It was at Spelman that I had my first black woman instructor; which is common here. I cannot even put into words how important it is for black women to be in an environment where the faculty and administration consists of black women, many of whom are Spelmanites themselves. I evolved so much through my matriculation at Spelman; especially in my confidence. I am so proud of the woman I am today, and I owe a lot of that to my experience at Spelman. I always said that if I have daughters they can go to any college they wish, but the one school I'm paying for is Spelman!"

Q "I absolutely love Spelman. **It is like no other**, and I would not trade my experience for the world!"

Q "When I applied to Spelman it was the only school I applied to, and if **I had to do it all over again, I would make the same choice**."

Q "**I would not trade my Spelman experience for anything**. If I had to do all over again, I would."

Q "I love Spelman and everything it stands for and everything it taught me. I would not be the woman I am if it had not of been for her! **The experience is like no other**, and you can't get it anywhere else."

Q "Overall, the Spelman experience, which included academics as well as extracurricular activities, helped prepare me to face the challenges of the real world. Oftentimes, it had me **juggling far more projects than the average person could manage**."

Q "Attending Spelman was **one of the best decisions that I ever made**."

Q "**I love Spelman, with all of its ups and downs**. My experience has been very positive."

Q "I think coming to Spelman and Atlanta was the best decision in my life. **I don't regret coming**."

Q "When I first came, I didn't want to go. I asked my mom to take me out. I wanted to go to Howard. I have this love for Howard, and I know I will go there for business or grad school. I am glad I got to go to Spelman, but at the end of the day, **I think I am more of a big-school girl**."

Q "I love Spelman. It has been a wonderful experience. I was nervous coming to an all-girls school because of females and drama. **It is the first place I have had the opportunity to form real friendships**. It's been great."

Q "So far so good. **I am really happy with my decision**. I am very happy to be among the people I get to interact with on a daily basis. I feel I will be a better person and only hope to give back a little of what it has been given to me."

Q "I absolutely love Spelman. I couldn't have pictured myself anywhere else, and **I believe this is the best decision I have made so far**."

Q "I wouldn't go anywhere else. **It is very diverse, even though it was all women**. I got to do a lot more than what I would have done up North. You have three other schools that you can take classes in."

The College Prowler Take On...
Overall Experience

Spelman students generally embrace both the good and the bad elements of their college experience and emerge with a positive overall view. The sisterhood, challenges, and nurturing environment are aspects of their time at Spelman that they cherish the most. Many express a love for Spelman that one could conclude transcends the educational experience and speaks more to a bond formed with the institution, the faculty, and their peers. Spelman is definitely a small school, so there are a few students who may feel like they missed out on the advantages of a big, coed, institution. For others, they like the fact that they had the access to the other campuses of the Atlanta University Center but were always able to return to the gates of Spelman.

Spelman is seen as a journey into womanhood for many young ladies. It is also an opportunity for many students to meet other women of color like themselves, for the first time in their lives. As was mentioned in the Diversity section, Spelman brings together a plethora of women who might not otherwise have met or ever discovered the common bonds they share despite their different upbringings and backgrounds. Academically, Spelman ranks high and has been recognized in the media for producing successful women who go on to be recognized in all fields of study, industry, and business.

The Inside Scoop

The Lowdown On...
The Inside Scoop

Spelman Slang:

Know the slang, know the school. The following is a list of things you really need to know before coming to Spelman. The more of these words you know, the better off you'll be.

The House – Another name for Morehouse College

The Yard – The grounds of the campus. Generally, the area in front of the Student Center. Usage: "I will see you on the Yard at Market Friday" In the past "the Yard" was also used to refer to Spelman's entire campus, as Morehouse was "the House."

House Man – A student of Morehouse

The Strip – The walkway on the way from Spelman to the Woodruff Library. "The Strip" is also sort of a borderline between Morehouse and Clark Atlanta University.

The AUC – Short reference to the Atlanta University Center and the schools in it

Spelmanite – Name for Spelman college student

Holla or hollah – Go talk to or approach as if to express a romantic interest

HH – Howard Harreld Hall

The Oval – Paved Circular area in the middle of campus

Cosby LL – Lower level of the Cosby Building

Stroll – Uniform walk performed by the Greeks. Usually done at parties or on the Yard.

The Grill – Fast food café in the Manley Center. Official name is the Jaguar Underground.

Lower Manley – Location of the SGA office, the Grill, and parts of Market Friday.

Club Woody – The Woodruff Library used by all of the schools in the AUC.

Set – A party. Usage: "Did you go to that set at Frequency the other night?"

Step or stepping – A series of movements involving, beats, rhythms, calls, and chants performed by members of Greek letter organizations. These can be done on an impromptu level, during step shows, or coming out/crossing shows.

ADW – African Diaspora & the World, a mandatory class for incoming students

Things I Wish I Knew Before Coming to Spelman

- Remember, most of the dorms do not have air conditioning. You will want to bring a fan.
- Bring a few suits for on-campus interviewing. Spelman has strong relationships with a number of Fortune 500 companies. You'll have many opportunities to score an internship, but you want to be able to dress the part.
- As off-the-wall as this might sound, bring a white dress. Spelman has a number of traditional ceremonies and activities which require that students wear white dresses. Tradition, even down to the outfit worn, is one of the major attractions of Spelman College.
- You will have a curfew during orientation week your first year at Spelman.
- The library is not on campus and is not open 24 hours a day.
- Atlanta does get cold in the winter, so don't underestimate the weather.

Tips to Succeed at Spelman

- Register early to get the good classes.
- Have a designated time to study and do homework.
- Talk to students who've had the "hard" teachers before for tips, notes, and advice.
- Take good notes in class.
- Read before class. Teachers like to call on students during discussions.
- Don't procrastinate on papers—remember, the computer lab is sometimes overrun during peak times.
- Bring a computer if you can.
- Go to a Spelman summer program to get a jump on things freshman year.

Spelman Urban Legends

- If you walk through the Alumnae Arch before your Class Day you won't graduate. (However, good luck finding anyone who will admit to walking through it prematurely!)
- Oprah only gives money to Morehouse.
- Only women have held the role of College president at Spelman.
- Spelman banned rap star Nelly from campus.
- Chadwick Hall, an old dorm that was demolished, was sinking into the ground and had become unsafe to live in.

School Spirit

School spirit is high, primarily during special events like Homecoming, Founders Week, Freshman Week, or graduation. You will always see students wearing Spelman paraphernalia. During your first week freshman year, you learn school songs and cheers, but other than the Spelman Hymn, you will probably never sing them again. Dorm spirit among first-year students is high as well. Each dorm is like its own little sorority, complete with Greek letter names and dorm colors. Unfortunately, all of this school spirit does not carry over to the sports arena. Go to any Spelman Jaguar game, and you'll find that the stands are far from full.

Traditions

Bench Ceremony
The Bench in this ceremony is located near the Alumnae Arch. The significance of the Bench is that it is only to be used by members of the current senior class. It is passed to the junior class on Class Day during graduation weekend. This ceremony dates back to 1941.

Freshman Traditions
Freshman Week is a tradition that stirs up the sisterhood of the incoming class, as well as the dorms. There are actually other traditions that first-year students will encounter, but to share them would diminish the special privilege of being a part of the Spelman family.

Ivy Oration
This is a speech given by the senior class valedictorian during Class Day, two days before graduation.

March Through the Arch
Spelman alumnae, wearing white dresses, lead the graduating class through the Alumnae Arch. This symbolizes their walk out of the gates of Spelman College and into the world.

Spelman Hymn
The Spelman Hymn was written by Eddye Mae Money Shivery a member of the class of 1934. It is sung at the conclusion of convocation and chapel events, as well as all alumnae events and chapter meetings.

The White Dress Tradition
One of the most well-known traditions involves a white dress and "flesh tone" stockings. This is sometimes referred to the "Spelman uniform" by students. Almost 100 years ago, there was an unwritten rule that Spelman students should have a "respectable and conservative" white dress. Students were also requested to own a pair of "sensible black shoes." In those days, this outfit promoted uniformity and signified the importance of most formal events. To this day, during special occasions, Spelman students and alumnae are requested to wear this outfit. During the new student induction ceremony, the Founders Day ceremony, and graduation, to name a few, you will see hundreds of women wearing white.

www.spelman.edu/reunion/whitedress.shtml

Finding a Job or Internship

The Lowdown On...
Finding a Job or Internship

Career Center:
Office of Career Planning and Development

Milligan Building, 2nd Floor
440 Westview Dr.

(404) 270-5273

Hours: Monday–Friday
9 a.m.–5 p.m.

Grads Entering the Job Market:
Within 6 Months: 52%
Within 1 Year: N/A

Services Available:
Career counseling

Company information sessions

eRecruiting

Graduate school preparatory programs

Mock interviews (mandatory if you interview through the school)

On-campus interviews

Resume and coverletter assistance

Advice

The Office of Career Placement and Development is a good option for finding summer internships and jobs after graduation, but don't limit yourself to this resource. Most students will say that networking plays a big part in getting the best opportunities. Also, career fairs are big in the AUC. The AUC sponsors one career fair every year that has a reputation for attracting Fortune 500 companies looking to hire Spelman students. Many times, companies send Spelman alumnae to schools in order to get recruits.

Make sure you stay abreast of the companies paying the career center a visit. You might also want to check out information sessions being held at surrounding schools. You might be able to make a good contact that can get you in the door. Sign up early for interviews, as the best companies get booked fast. Once you are in for an interview, don't mess up your chances by showing up late or canceling at the last minute. Not only will you burn the bridge with the company, but unless it was an emergency, the career center may prohibit you from signing up for additional interviews.

Keep your eyes open for Spelman alumnae that work for companies that you are interested in. The sisterly support is there both inside and outside of the gates, and chances are, if a company is already pleased with the alumni of a particular school, they will be interested in hiring more.

Firms That Most Frequently Hire Grads

Abbott Laboratories, AT Kearney, Bank of America, Bank of New York, Baxter Health Care, Chase, Federal Reserve Bank, Goldman Sachs, Kimberly Clark, Merk, Merrill Lynch, Morgan Stanley

Alumnae

The Lowdown On...
Alumnae

Web Sites:
Alumnae Programs & Services
www.spelman.edu/alumnae/services

AUC Alumni Association
www.aucalumni.com

National Alumnae Association of Spelman College
www.naasc.org

Alumnae Giving Rate:
18%

Offices:
National Alumnae Association of Spelman College (NAASC)
PO Box 42828
Atlanta
info@naasc.org

Office of Institutional Advancement
(404) 270-5047

Alumnae Publications:
The Spelman Messenger

Services Available

The SpelAgent Program allows alumnae to assist with fundraising, reunion planning and donor identification. There is also the Alumnae-Student Exchange which creates an avenue for alumnae to share tips on careers and leadership. Additionally, there is an Alumnae Career Network and groups for alumnae that focus on Homecoming, Founders Day, and Reunion.

The NAASC supports chapters in major cities across the United States. The chapters help by spearheading fundraisers in local areas for scholarships and providing a local network of Spelman alumnae so that women may continue to celebrate the sisterhood outside of the gates.

AUCAlumni.com is an site created by alumni and friends of the Atlanta University Center, including Spelman. Here you can read about notable alumni, find out about events, and also search jobs.

Major Alumnae Events

Alumnae Achievement Awards
This is an invitation-only breakfast at Tiffany & Co. during which alumnae are honored in the areas of arts and media, business and law, civic service, education, and health and sciences.

Homecoming
Homecoming is one of the most anticipated events of the year. Coronation of Ms. Spelman and her court, guest speakers, and other on-campus activities are part of this weekend. Highlights of the weekend include celebrity concerts, the step show, tailgating, the Morehouse football game, and parties!

Reunion
During graduation weekend in May, Spelman alumnae return to campus for Reunion Weekend. Everyone is invited to attend, and there are generally class-specific activities, seminars, a luncheon, and a banquet for all to attend.

Did You Know?

Famous Spelman Alumnae:

Mattiwilda Dobbs Janzon (Class of '46) – First African American to perform opera at La Scala

LaTanya Richardson Jackson (Class of '71) – Stage, film and television actress seen in the films *The Fighting Temptations*, *Macolm X*, and *U.S. Marshals*, and TV shows *NYPD Blue*, *Ally McBeal*, and *Boston Public*

Varnette Honeywood (Class of '72) – Artist and creator of the Little Bill character in the book series written by Bill Cosby

Kathleen McGee-Anderson (Class of '72) – Television producer and playwright. Consulting producer for Showtime television series *Soul Food*

Iris Little Thomas (Class of '79) – Actress seen in *Everyday People* and *Boycott*

Shaun Robinson (Class of '80) – Actress and correspondent for *Access Hollywood*

Rolanda Watts (Class of '80) – Talk show host, guest star on *The Bold & The Beautiful* and *West Wing*

Sherri A. McGee (Class of '87) – Co-author *Skinny Women are Evil: Notes of a BIG GIRL in a Small-Minded World* with actress Mo'Nique

Tayari Jones (Class of '91) – Author of *Leaving Atlanta*

Tanika Ray (Class of '94) – Host of *Head 2 Toe* on Lifetime

Reisha L. Raney (Class of '95) – Appeared on reality show *Hooking Up* on ABC

Stephanie Scott (Class of '98) – Associate beauty editor for *Essence* magazine

Keisha Knight-Pulliam (Class of '01) – Actress, noted for her role in *The Cosby Show*

Danica Tisdale (Class of '01) – Miss Georgia 2004, the first African American to be crowned

Lia Hackerson, April Hanks, and Valerie Fountaine (Class of '99) – Three Spelman women chosen to appear on *Trading Spaces*

Student Organizations

ABLE – Trains students to be mentors to students at nearby public schools

Afrakete – Group in support of gay and bisexual students

Alabaster Box – Club that seeks to glorify God

Al-Nissa – Support group for Muslim women

Alpha Epsilon Delta – Honor Society for pre-med students

Alpha Lambda Delta – Honor Society for first year students

Alpha Kappa Alpha, Inc. – *www.sweetmupi.com*

Alpha Sigma Lambda – Honor Society for students in the Spelman College Gateway Program

Association for Computing Machinery

Atlanta Adventist Collegiate Society

AUC Baha'i Club

AUC Council of Students – Promote unity between AUC schools

Beta Kappa Chi – Scientific Honor Society

The Biology Club

The California Club

Campus Crusade for Christ

The Chemistry Club

Class Councils – Made up of representatives from each class

Crossfire International Campus Ministry

The Dark Tower Project – Club for artists

Delaware Club

Delta Sigma Theta, Inc. – *www.geocities.com/etakappadst*

Diverge Art Club

The Economics Club

The English Club

Environmental Task Force

Feminist Majority Leadership Alliance

The French Club

The Georgia Club

Golden Key International Honor Society

The Grandaughters Club – For students who have had a mother or aunt attend

Happiness In Praise for His Overflowing Presence – College campus bible study

The Health Careers Club

Honda Campus All-Star Challenge – prepares students for tournaments

House of Representatives – This group assists the SGA by working with other student organizations and clubs.

Illinois Club

InterVarsity Christian Fellowship

The International Students Organization

The Japanese Club

Kappa Delta Epsilon – Honor Society

The Massachusetts Club

The Mathematics Club

Media Arts Society of Spelman

Mortar Board Senior Honor Society

Movements of Praise Dance Team

The Ohio Club

National Association for the Advancement of Colored People (NAACP)

National Society of Black Engineers

National Society of Collegiate Scholars

The Newman Organization – Group for Catholic students

The Outlet – Spiritual club

Peer Education Program (PEPers) – Sponsor events and provide support around healthy relationships, self image, etc.

Phi Beta Kappa Honor Society

Philanthropy Council

The Philosophy Society

The Physics Club

Pi Sigma Alpha Political Science Honor Society

Pre-Alumnae Council – Attend events that assist with fundraising

The Pre-Law Society – Joint club with Morehouse students

The Pre-Theology Society

Psi Chi National Honor Society in Psychology

Resident Assistant Council

The Rotaract Club – Joint club with Morehouse that fosters relationships based on service

SisterFire Collective – Focused on self empowerment

Sociological and Anthropological Sisterhood: Scholar Activists for Reshaping Attitudes at Spelman (SASSAFRAS) – Social action group

Spelman College Jazz Ensemble

Spelman College Glee Club

Spelman Student Government Association – Student-elected leaders who govern the school under the guidance of faculty and staff.

Spriggs-Burroughs Ensemble – Theater and performing arts

Students in Free Enterprise

Student Georgia Association of Educators

Sigma Alpha Iota Music Fraternity

Sigma Tau Delta International English Honor Society

Sister Steps – Mentorship program for inner city youth

Student Health Associates and Peer Educators (SHAPE)

Students for the Preservation of Sisterhood (SPS)

Taking Responsibility To Understand Each Other (TRUE) – Club that supports the support of students with disabilities

The Tennessee Club

The Texas Club

The Tri State Club

Toni Cade Bambara Scholar Activists – Group that supports the feminist movement

Upsilon Pi Epsilon Honor Society for the Computing Sciences

Zeta Phi Beta Sorority, Inc.

The Best & Worst

The Ten BEST Things About Spelman

1. Homecoming
2. In the heart of the Atlanta University Center
3. Unique traditions that are a part of the rich history of the school
4. Market Friday
5. The Grill
6. Freshman Week
7. ADW (but you won't think that until after you graduate)
8. The sisterhood and friends you will make
9. Academic and social organizations (the Greeks!)
10. Graduation! You will cry, but it is one of the most touching experiences you will ever have.

The Ten WORST Things About Spelman

1. Your car getting towed off campus
2. Parking sucks!
3. Dorms with no air conditioning
4. Controlled male visitation
5. Convocation—mandatory for freshmen
6. The gym at Read Hall
7. Crowded computer labs
8. ADW—You will hate it while you are there.
9. No cars allowed for freshmen
10. The cost (it can be an expensive education!)

Visiting

The Lowdown On...
Visiting

Hotel Information:

Airport:
Westin Atlanta Airport
4736 Best Rd.
(404) 762-7676
www.westin.com
Distance from Campus: 10 miles
Price: $109–$299

Downtown:
AmeriSuites
330 Peachtree St., Downtown
(404) 577-1980
www.amerisuites.com
Distance from Campus: Less than 8 miles
Price: $99–$130

Marriot Marquis
265 Peachtree Center Ave.
(404) 521-0000
www.marriot.com
Distance from Campus: Less than 8 miles
Price Range: $149–$240

Omni Hotel at CNN Center
100 CNN Center, Downtown
(404) 659-0000
www.omnihotels.com
Distance from Campus: Less than 5 miles
Price Range: $149–$389

Midtown:
Sheraton Colony Square
188 14th St., Midtown
(404) 892-66000
Distance from Campus: Less than 10 miles
Price: $99–$199

West End:
The Castleberry Inn
186 Northside Dr., West End
(404) 893-4663
www.castleberryinn.com
Distance from Campus: Less than a mile
Price: $62–$150

Schedule a Group Information Session or Interview

Interviews can be set up with local alumnae or an admissions counselor by contacting the Office of Admission.

(800) 982-2411

(404) 270-5193

E-Mail: admiss@spelman.edu

Campus Tours

The college supports group tours and individual tours. You can book a tour online, just look for the link on the page for prospective students. Book early, because the dates do fill up. Tours are Monday through Friday starting at 10 a.m. and 2 p.m. Wear comfortable shoes because it is a walking tour and will last about an hour. During the tour, you will also stop by the admissions office.

Overnight Visits

Spel-Bound Program

The Spel-Bound program provides the opportunity for prospective students who have been extended the invitation to enroll at the college. It is two days in length and prospective students have the opportunity to stay with a Spelman student and experience a day of classes. Parents are also invited to attend some of the program activities. Call the Office of Admission for more information.

Directions to Campus

Driving from the North.
- Take I-85 South to I-20 West.
- From I-20 West Exit at (#55 B) Lee St.
- Turn right at Lee St.
- Go through one traffic light (Westview Dr.).
- After passing large parking lot, make a right into driveway.
- Drive straight to the gate of Spelman College.

Driving from the South
- Take 85 North to I-20 West.
- From I-20 West Exit at (#55 B) Lee St.
- Turn right at Lee St.
- Go through one traffic light (Westview Dr.).
- After passing large parking lot, make a right into driveway.
- Drive straight to the gate of Spelman College.

Driving from the East
- Take I-20 West Exit at (#55 B) Lee St.
- Turn right at Lee St.
- Go through one traffic light (Westview Dr.).
- After passing large parking lot, make a right into driveway.
- Drive straight to the gate of Spelman College.

Driving from the West
- Take I-20 East.
- From I-20 East Exit at (#55 A) Lowery Blvd.
- Cross Lowery Blvd and remain on Oak St.
- When you get to Lee St. make a left.
- Go through two traffic lights.
- After passing large parking lot, make a right into driveway.
- Drive straight to the gate of Spelman College.

Words to Know

Academic Probation – A suspension imposed on a student if he or she fails to keep up with the school's minimum academic requirements. Those unable to improve their grades after receiving this warning can face dismissal.

Beer Pong/Beirut – A drinking game involving cups of beer arranged in a pyramid shape on each side of a table. The goal is to get a ping pong ball into one of the opponent's cups by throwing the ball or hitting it with a paddle. If the ball lands in a cup, the opponent is required to drink the beer.

Bid – An invitation from a fraternity or sorority to 'pledge' (join) that specific house.

Blue-Light Phone – Brightly-colored phone posts with a blue light bulb on top. These phones exist for security purposes and are located at various outside locations around most campuses. In an emergency, a student can pick up one of these phones (free of charge) to connect with campus police or a security escort.

Campus Police – Police who are specifically assigned to a given institution. Campus police are typically not regular city officers; they are employed by the university in a full-time capacity.

Club Sports – A level of sports that falls somewhere between varsity and intramural. If a student is unable to commit to a varsity team but has a lot of passion for athletics, a club sport could be a better, less intense option. Even less demanding, intramural (IM) sports often involve no traveling and considerably less time.

Cocaine – An illegal drug. Also known as "coke" or "blow," cocaine often resembles a white crystalline or powdery substance. It is highly addictive and dangerous.

Common Application – An application with which students can apply to multiple schools.

Course Registration – The period of official class selection for the upcoming quarter or semester. Prior to registration, it is best to prepare several back-up courses in case a particular class becomes full. If a course is full, students can place themselves on the waitlist, although this still does not guarantee entry.

Division Athletics – Athletic classifications range from Division I to Division III. Division IA is the most competitive, while Division III is considered to be the least competitive.

Dorm – A dorm (or dormitory) is an on-campus housing facility. Dorms can provide a range of options from suite-style rooms to more communal options that include shared bathrooms. Most first-year students live in dorms. Some upperclassmen who wish to stay on campus also choose this option.

Early Action – An application option with which a student can apply to a school and receive an early acceptance response without a binding commitment. This system is becoming less and less available.

Early Decision – An application option that students should use only if they are certain they plan to attend the school in question. If a student applies using the early decision option and is admitted, he or she is required and bound to attend that university. Admission rates are usually higher among students who apply through early decision, as the student is clearly indicating that the school is his or her first choice.

Ecstasy – An illegal drug. Also known as "E" or "X," ecstasy looks like a pill and most resembles an aspirin. Considered a party drug, ecstasy is very dangerous and can be deadly.

Ethernet – An extremely fast Internet connection available in most university-owned residence halls. To use an Ethernet connection properly, a student will need a network card and cable for his or her computer.

Fake ID – A counterfeit identification card that contains false information. Most commonly, students get fake IDs with altered birthdates so that they appear to be older than 21 (and therefore of legal drinking age). Even though it is illegal, many college students have fake IDs in hopes of purchasing alcohol or getting into bars.

Frosh – Slang for "freshman" or "freshmen."

Hazing – Initiation rituals administered by some fraternities or sororities as part of the pledging process. Many universities have outlawed hazing due to its degrading, and sometimes dangerous, nature.

Intramurals (IMs) – A popular, and usually free, sport league in which students create teams and compete against one another. These sports vary in competitiveness and can include a range of activities—everything from billiards to water polo. IM sports are a great way to meet people with similar interests.

Keg – Officially called a half-barrel, a keg contains roughly 200 12-ounce servings of beer.

LSD – An illegal drug, also known as acid, this hallucinogenic drug most commonly resembles a tab of paper.

Marijuana – An illegal drug, also known as weed or pot; along with alcohol, marijuana is one of the most commonly-found drugs on campuses across the country.

Major –The focal point of a student's college studies; a specific topic that is studied for a degree. Examples of majors include physics, English, history, computer science, economics, business, and music. Many students decide on a specific major before arriving on campus, while others are simply "undecided" until declaring a major. Those who are extremely interested in two areas can also choose to double major.

Meal Block – The equivalent of one meal. Students on a meal plan usually receive a fixed number of meals per week. Each meal, or "block," can be redeemed at the school's dining facilities in place of cash. Often, a student's weekly allotment of meal blocks will be forfeited if not used.

Minor – An additional focal point in a student's education. Often serving as a complement or addition to a student's main area of focus, a minor has fewer requirements and prerequisites to fulfill than a major. Minors are not required for graduation from most schools; however some students who want to explore many different interests choose to pursue both a major and a minor.

Mushrooms – An illegal drug. Also known as "'shrooms," this drug resembles regular mushrooms but is extremely hallucinogenic.

Off-Campus Housing – Housing from a particular landlord or rental group that is not affiliated with the university. Depending on the college, off-campus housing can range from extremely popular to non-existent. Students who choose to live off campus are typically given more freedom, but they also have to deal with possible subletting scenarios, furniture, bills, and other issues. In addition to these factors, rental prices and distance often affect a student's decision to move off campus.

Office Hours – Time that teachers set aside for students who have questions about coursework. Office hours are a good forum for students to go over any problems and to show interest in the subject material.

Pledging – The early phase of joining a fraternity or sorority, pledging takes place after a student has gone through rush and received a bid. Pledging usually lasts between one and two semesters. Once the pledging period is complete and a particular student has done everything that is required to become a member, that student is considered a brother or sister. If a fraternity or a sorority would decide to "haze" a group of students, this initiation would take place during the pledging period.

Private Institution – A school that does not use tax revenue to subsidize education costs. Private schools typically cost more than public schools and are usually smaller.

Prof – Slang for "professor."

Public Institution – A school that uses tax revenue to subsidize education costs. Public schools are often a good value for in-state residents and tend to be larger than most private colleges.

Quarter System (or Trimester System) – A type of academic calendar system. In this setup, students take classes for three academic periods. The first quarter usually starts in late September or early October and concludes right before Christmas. The second quarter usually starts around early to mid–January and finishes up around March or April. The last academic quarter, or "third quarter," usually starts in late March or early April and finishes up in late May or Mid-June. The fourth quarter is summer. The major difference between the quarter system and semester system is that students take more, less comprehensive courses under the quarter calendar.

RA (Resident Assistant) – A student leader who is assigned to a particular floor in a dormitory in order to help to the other students who live there. An RA's duties include ensuring student safety and providing assistance wherever possible.

Recitation – An extension of a specific course; a review session. Some classes, particularly large lectures, are supplemented with mandatory recitation sessions that provide a relatively personal class setting.

Rolling Admissions – A form of admissions. Most commonly found at public institutions, schools with this type of policy continue to accept students throughout the year until their class sizes are met. For example, some schools begin accepting students as early as December and will continue to do so until April or May.

Room and Board – This figure is typically the combined cost of a university-owned room and a meal plan.

Room Draw/Housing Lottery – A common way to pick on-campus room assignments for the following year. If a student decides to remain in university-owned housing, he or she is assigned a unique number that, along with seniority, is used to determine his or her housing for the next year.

Rush – The period in which students can meet the brothers and sisters of a particular chapter and find out if a given fraternity or sorority is right for them. Rushing a fraternity or a sorority is not a requirement at any school. The goal of rush is to give students who are serious about pledging a feel for what to expect.

Semester System – The most common type of academic calendar system at college campuses. This setup typically includes two semesters in a given school year. The fall semester starts around the end of August or early September and concludes before winter vacation. The spring semester usually starts in mid-January and ends in late April or May.

Student Center/Rec Center/Student Union – A common area on campus that often contains study areas, recreation facilities, and eateries. This building is often a good place to meet up with fellow students; depending on the school, the student center can have a huge role or a non-existent role in campus life.

Student ID – A university-issued photo ID that serves as a student's key to school-related functions. Some schools require students to show these cards in order to get into dorms, libraries, cafeterias, and other facilities. In addition to storing meal plan information, in some cases, a student ID can actually work as a debit card and allow students to purchase things from bookstores or local shops.

Suite – A type of dorm room. Unlike dorms that feature communal bathrooms shared by the entire floor, suites offer bathrooms shared only among the suite. Suite-style dorm rooms can house anywhere from two to ten students.

TA (Teacher's Assistant) – An undergraduate or grad student who helps in some manner with a specific course. In some cases, a TA will teach a class, assist a professor, grade assignments, or conduct office hours.

Undergraduate – A student in the process of studying for his or her bachelor's degree.

About the Author

Ms. Tiffani "T." Murray is a graduate of Spelman College and the Georgia Institute of Technology. She is currently a project manager with Capgemini in Atlanta. Her projects have allowed her to author and direct two company-wide human resources videos and provide content for the North American internal newsletter. She has also co-authored and designed participant and facilitator guides for internal training focused on creativity, communication, and problem solving.

A published author, Ms. Murray's work has appeared in a number of print publications. She has submitted biographies to the *African American National Biography*, and she was also published in the 2004 anthology *Delta Girls: Stories of Sisterhood*. She is a staff writer for *AUC Magazine* and the co-founder and director of communications and special events for *AUCAlumni.com*. She is also the managing editor of *AUCAlumni.com*'s online news site. T. Murray has interviewed and written feature articles on such celebrities as Sheri McGee, Kathleen McGhee Anderson, and Bryan-Michael Cox. In 2000, she was published as an anonymous writer in the *Wetfeet.com* insider guide to Cap, Gemini, Ernst & Young. As a contract profile writer for *Match.com*, she also gained a wealth of knowledge about the world of dating through her interviews with a number of subscribers. Her work with Match inspired her to write her first non-fiction book, *Stuck on Stupid: A Guide for Today's Single Woman Stuck in Yesterday's Stupid Relationships*. She is currently working on self-publishing *SOS* and her debut novel, *Group Project*, both to be released in 2006. A freelance writer, Ms. Murray's work has been featured on Internet sites such as *MinorityProfessionalNetwork.com*.

In addition to consulting for one of the original "Big 5," Ms. Murray spends her spare time planning events and was a co-chair on the planning committee for the 2005 Turner Broadcasting Systems Trumpet Awards in Atlanta. She is the daughter of Joseph and Clara Murray who reside in Hampton, VA and sister of LaTondra Murray, PhD, of Durham, NC.

T. Murray
tiffanimurray@collegeprowler.com

California Colleges

**California dreamin'?
This book is a must have for you!**

CALIFORNIA COLLEGES
7¼" X 10", 762 Pages Paperback
$29.95 Retail
1-59658-501-3

Stanford, UC Berkeley, Caltech—California is home to some of America's greatest institutes of higher learning. *California Colleges* gives the lowdown on 24 of the best, side by side, in one prodigious volume.

New England Colleges

**Looking for peace in the Northeast?
Pick up this regional guide to New England!**

NEW ENGLAND COLLEGES
7¼" X 10", 1015 Pages Paperback
$29.95 Retail
1-59658-504-8

New England is the birthplace of many prestigious universities, and with so many to choose from, picking the right school can be a tough decision. With inside information on over 34 competive Northeastern schools, *New England Colleges* provides the same high-quality information prospective students expect from College Prowler in one all-inclusive, easy-to-use reference.

Schools of the South

Headin' down south? This book will help you find your way to the perfect school!

SCHOOLS OF THE SOUTH
7¼" X 10", 773 Pages Paperback
$29.95 Retail
1-59658-503-X

Southern pride is always strong. Whether it's across town or across state, many Southern students are devoted to their home sweet home. *Schools of the South* offers an honest student perspective on 36 universities available south of the Mason-Dixon.

Untangling the Ivy League

The ultimate book for everything Ivy!

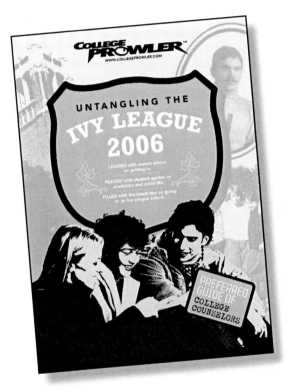

UNTANGLING THE IVY LEAGUE
7¼" X 10", 567 Pages Paperback
$24.95 Retail
1-59658-500-5

Ivy League students, alumni, admissions officers, and other top insiders get together to tell it like it is. *Untangling the Ivy League* covers every aspect—from admissions and athletics to secret societies and urban legends—of the nation's eight oldest, wealthiest, and most competitive colleges and universities.

Need Help Paying For School?
Apply for our scholarship!

College Prowler awards thousands of dollars a year to students who compose the best essays. E-mail scholarship@collegeprowler.com for more information, or call 1-800-290-2682.

Apply now at **www.collegeprowler.com**

Tell Us What Life Is Really Like at Your School!

Have you ever wanted to let people know what your college is really like? Now's your chance to help millions of high school students choose the right college.

Let your voice be heard.

Check out **www.collegeprowler.com** for more info!

Need More Help?

Do you have more questions about this school? Can't find a certain statistic? College Prowler is here to help. We are the best source of college information out there. We have a network of thousands of students who can get the latest information on any school to you ASAP. E-mail us at info@collegeprowler.com with your college-related questions.

E-Mail Us Your College-Related Questions!

Check out **www.collegeprowler.com** for more details.
1-800-290-2682

Write For Us!
Get published! Voice your opinion.

Writing a College Prowler guidebook is both fun and rewarding; our open-ended format allows your own creativity free reign. Our writers have been featured in national newspapers and have seen their names in bookstores across the country. Now is your chance to break into the publishing industry with one of the country's fastest-growing publishers!

Apply now at **www.collegeprowler.com**

Contact editor@collegeprowler.com or
call 1-800-290-2682 for more details.

Pros and Cons

Still can't figure out if this is the right school for you? You've already read through this in-depth guide; why not list the pros and cons? It will really help with narrowing down your decision and determining whether or not this school is right for you.

Pros	Cons
....	....
....	....
....	....
....	....
....	....
....	....
....	....
....	....
....	....
....	....
....	....
....	....
....	....

Pros and Cons

Still can't figure out if this is the right school for you? You've already read through this in-depth guide; why not list the pros and cons? It will really help with narrowing down your decision and determining whether or not this school is right for you.

Pros	**Cons**
....	....
....	....
....	....
....	....
....	....
....	....
....	....
....	....
....	....
....	....
....	....
....	....
....	....
....	....

Notes

Notes

Notes

Notes

Notes

Notes

Notes

Notes

Notes

Notes

Notes

Notes

Notes

Notes

Notes